LOCUS

TAKE CONTROL AND CHANGE
THE DIRECTION OF YOUR LIFE

SUZY SIEGLE

Copyright © 2022 by Suzy Siegle
All rights reserved.

Although the publisher and the author have made every effort to ensure that the information in this book was correct at press time and while this publication is designed to provide accurate information in regard to the subject matter covered, the publisher and the author assume no responsibility for errors, inaccuracies, omissions, or any other inconsistencies herein and hereby disclaim any liability to any party for any loss, damage, or disruption caused by errors or omissions, whether such errors or omissions result from negligence, accident, or any other cause. The content in this book is meant to inform and not to be construed as advice for career advancement or specific business outcomes.

ISBN paperback: 979-8-9867810-0-6
ISBN ebook: 979-8-9867810-1-3
ISBN audiobook: 979-8-9867810-2-0

Duttweiler's Internal Control Index
is reprinted in this book by permission of SAGE Publications, Inc.:

Duttweiler, P.C. The Internal Control Index: A Newly Developed Measure of Locus of Control. Educational and Psychological Measurement 44(2), pp. 209-221. Copyright © 1984 by Educational and Psychological Measurement.

Published by Locus Mindset® LLC.

> "In this short life
> That only lasts an hour
> How much—how little—is
> Within our power?"
>
> —Emily Dickinson

CONTENTS

Introduction	7
1. Our Locus of Control	13
2. The Subconscious Mind: The Seat of Our Locus of Control	29
3. The Power of Early Experiences I: Perception versus Reality	41
4. The Power of Early Experiences II: Our Survival Instinct	53
5. Reshaping Our Memories to Free Our Minds	67
6. The Connection Between Mind and Body	89
7. The THRIVE Framework: Taking Back Control	111
Epilogue. The Tapestry of Life	129
Duttweiler's Internal Control Index	133
The THRIVE Journal	137
Sample Template for the Nightly THRIVE Framework	139
Sample Template for Morning Mindset Mastery	140
Endnotes	141
About the Author	149

INTRODUCTION

Patterns. How many times do we repeat patterns in our lives? Or relive the same scene, situation, or event, over and over again? And how often are we completely unaware of what we are doing and why we keep doing it (and why we keep getting the same results, good or bad)?

In high school, I loved watching *Star Trek: The Next Generation*. Ostensibly about space exploration, the series actually focused on multilayered life lessons and the interpersonal relationships among the crew members. Their adventures in space paralleled the personal growth and evolution of the characters.

In one episode, aptly named "Cause and Effect," the crew kept reliving the same day. Several of them noticed feelings of déjà vu and mentioned having the strange feeling that the experiences they were living through seemed eerily familiar. Yet they were unable to recall why or understand how. The episode ended with the starship exploding in space, everyone dying, and then awakening to repeat the same day, *again*.

Finally, the crew discovers that the ship is stuck in a "temporal causality loop," or time loop. They also realize that each time the loop begins, they lose all conscious memory of the day before. Without the knowledge of how to escape, they could be doomed to repeat the same decisions and keep reliving the same day forever. Finally, the crew figures out how to send themselves a message, a "clue," that isn't dependent upon retaining their conscious memory, and they eventually escape the loop.

For some reason, this episode resonated with me. I wondered if the same thing happens to us? Do we get stuck in our own temporal causality loop and repeat similar experiences in our lives, over and over again, without being aware of how to change our direction and escape the cycle?

These patterns may be about money. We might get a promotion, increase our income, or resolve to build our savings, only to find we are still spending more, saving less, and unable to escape the never-ending hamster wheel of debt. Or perhaps it's the same argument with a family member or our partner that replays time and time again, like a record stuck on a turntable. Maybe it's the New Year's resolution we make, and soon break, to eat healthier or get in better shape.

It's easy to point to external factors for why these patterns happen, such as time, work, or family commitments. And, at the same time, we may have this nagging feeling that some force within us may be sabotaging our desired outcome. On the surface, however, we only see the same pattern repeating. These patterns play a valuable role in giving us clues to a deeper reality. They tell us what is happening underneath the surface—beneath our conscious awareness and actions.

For years, I noticed these repetitive patterns in my own life. By most external measures, my career looked like a successful one that integrated several areas of expertise: law, business, and higher education. After college, I went to law school, then earned a doctorate, and then an MBA. With each degree under my belt, I was convinced I would finally feel as if I were smart enough. Yet, I would inevitably feel that I still wasn't good enough. Thus, once again, I would pursue another credential to fill that void. The truth was that the feeling of being "enough" wasn't connected to more education. It was connected to a much deeper sense of self-worth that I had yet to uncover and resolve.

In relationships, I repeated the same patterns. With each new partner, I was sure I'd found that ideal, you-complete-me relationship. And, when that feeling of completeness did not automatically appear, or when I perceived it to fade over time, I would leave the relationship and quickly enter a new one. Much like with the degrees, this sense of completeness was not something anyone else could give to me; it was something I had to create for myself.

And, finally, there was my health. In high school, I became addicted to exercising, eating low-fat foods, and eliminating most sugars, obsessed with attaining optimal health. Of course, as with many patterns throughout my life, I tended to go to extremes. So much so that my period stopped for two years because I reached such a low body weight. I planned my food each day and ate just enough not to feel tired or run down for my workouts, but I clearly had an unhealthy relationship with food, health, and my own body.

With all of this turmoil came a high sense of anxiety and a fear of losing control. And, at the same time, I was comforted by the feeling that, somehow, I had more control over my life and the results I was seeing within it. The truth was that I was stuck in a self-destructive pattern.

This is the book that I wish someone had given to me 20 years ago. It is the book that would have explained my deeply-rooted fear of being unworthy and never being enough. It's the book that would have helped me better understand how I could claim more control over my life so I could stop repeating these painful patterns.

Of course, the irony is that without experiencing those patterns, I wouldn't have been able to write this book now. And so, my hope is that this can help others who may be feeling as if they're reliving the same day over and over again, and who have this nagging awareness that they might have the power to change this destructive cycle, if only they knew how.

This book explains how we can gain more control over key areas of our lives: health, wealth, and relationships. While this is not an academic work, I include references to compelling research, articles, studies, and thought leadership that span cognitive and positive psychology, neuroscience and neuropsychology, memory reconsolidation and trauma, and much more. Note that all the articles and peer-reviewed studies showing the results I cite are gathered in the Endnotes section at the back of this book so you may pursue further reading.

I also include tools and a framework—specifically the THRIVE framework—that I've developed and used to gain more control and implement positive changes. And I've created a THRIVE journal that includes the framework and accompanying journal pages to support you in the process, available separately on Amazon. I will wait to explain the THRIVE framework in a later chapter because the information leading up to it helps to lay the foundation and provide the explanation for how and why THRIVE works.

I've also found these tools to be incredibly useful in my professional roles as an educator and leader, and I think they have huge relevance in business and for entrepreneurs. So much of what leaders struggle with stems from personal challenges deep within themselves. And, while there's no shortage of leadership development books, workshops, and seminars, many tend to focus on more conscious leadership development strategies, tactics, and attributes. I wish there were more resources that focus on the personal growth and development of leaders from the inside out.

Leadership development *is* personal development. It's a journey to the center of ourselves and back again. And it impacts every area of our lives. Leadership is not only a position or title one holds. We are all leaders in the way in which we show up every day and how we govern our own actions and reactions. In essence, our self-leadership. Therefore, you don't have to be in a formal leadership role to work on your own leadership development. Self-leadership is our way of being. It's how we move through the world, and it touches on answers to some of these questions:

- How do we show up at work and with others?
- Do we get defensive, offended, or emotionally triggered?
- What type of energy do we bring into the room?
- Are we repeating damaging patterns that create toxic work environments?
- Do we blame others for our mistakes or inability to deliver results?

The truth is that all the different parts of our lives are connected, whether we realize it or not. When we are feeling stressed and overwhelmed at work, our health and relationships are negatively impacted. When our relationships are in trouble, this adversely affects our health and our job.

By isolating and addressing harmful patterns in one area, we are helping ourselves to drive change and thrive in *all* areas. But what is it that really drives these patterns? Our behavior patterns are connected to a mechanism deep inside all of us that controls what we perceive, how we feel, and how we act and react to ourselves and the world around us—our locus of control. They key to understanding how it works and how it plays such an important role in our lives will be the focus of this book.

I'll explain what locus of control is and how, by mastering it, we can gain greater control and achieve better outcomes in every area of our lives. This book is not just for business leaders or those in organizational leadership. It is for entrepreneurs, counselors, life coaches, driven professionals, and those who have struggled to overcome negative patterns. It's for those who want to learn how to take control and change the direction of their life!

CHAPTER 1

OUR LOCUS OF CONTROL

The inspiration for this book came from one simple question: In any given day, what percentage of your actions, decisions, and circumstances are within your control?

The answer is complicated. Let me explain. About a decade ago, I began studying the concept of locus of control. I had come across an article talking about the importance of hiring employees who possessed an internal locus of control. In brief, it meant they believed they were in control of events in their lives.

Not knowing what that meant, I began researching it. Something about this concept was attractive to me. On some level, I had this awareness that I was more in control of the outcomes I saw in my life. And, at the same time, there was so much that felt beyond my control and more automatic in nature, like my feelings, emotional reactions, and perceptions about others and myself. I'd always found it so empowering to believe we could be more in control of our lives. At the same time, I felt a bit unsettled at how to make sense of a world in which so much felt beyond my control.

ARE YOU AN INTERNAL OR AN EXTERNAL?

In 1954, psychologist Julian Rotter put forth the theory of locus of control. He suggested two tendencies for how people *believe* and *perceive* their lives are controlled. Dr. Rotter classified those who believe *they* are responsible for the results and outcomes in their lives as *internals,* or those who have an internal locus (i.e., location) of control. He classified those who believe that luck, chance, circumstance, or "powerful others" are responsible for the outcomes and results in their lives as *externals,* or people who have an external locus of control.

In other words, an internal believes that they are the author of their own life. They take ownership of mistakes and setbacks, and they take responsibility for their decisions and successes. Rather than blame others or life's circumstances, they focus on what they can do to improve and thrive. An external believes other people, external environmental factors, and chance exert greater control over their experiences and decisions, so they take little responsibility for what happens in their lives, positive or negative.

During my career, I've had the opportunity to lead and participate in various hiring committees. As I became more interested in this concept of locus of control, I began to ask candidates what I would call "the locus question":

> "Thinking about any given day in your life, from the moment you wake up until you go to bed, what percentage of your actions, decisions, and circumstances are within your control?"

I posed this question during every interview I was a part of, and the results were surprising. Some people were completely taken aback. It certainly was not your standard interview fare. One person grew visibly agitated and asked me if I was asking if she was a "control freak." She went on to say that she was not a micromanager but an empowering supervisor. While this was great information to know, she ultimately didn't answer the question.

In another interview, a candidate slyly said 10 percent. He said he really didn't believe we have much control over our day, and that he had learned to roll with the punches and think on his feet. Several other candidates mused about the question, circled around it, or opined that they didn't have control over traffic or the weather.

Of the ones who did answer, many gave numbers that ranged from 10 to 50%. I've even had a colleague on the interview committee follow me into the hallway after the interview, ask me what I was trying to find out with this question, and tell me that she wasn't sure how she would have answered it.

Yet, a few people who were comfortable with the question promptly answered in the high 80 to 90% range. "While I may not control everything around me, I certainly have full control over my actions, reactions, and decisions," said one woman who was ultimately offered the job and turned out to be an outstanding hire.

There seemed to be one thing in common among all the interviewees. They all appeared to have an initial, intuitive response. It was as if, on some subconscious level, they knew or felt the answer. Yet there was some sort of filter, or a checks-and-balances process taking place in their minds. This question offered a window into their own locus of control. There was no right answer. Yet it gave some insight into where they believed the agency for their decisions and results resided, and thus how they would act and react in certain situations. For example, if they had a big project at work and needed to meet a deadline, would they take responsibility for the outcome and find a way to succeed, or would they blame others if they didn't deliver?

INTERNALS AND POSITIVE LIFE OUTCOMES

Since Dr. Rotter's initial publication, numerous studies have indicated a positive correlation between an internal locus of control and achieving better outcomes in major life areas: money, relationships, work, health, and overall well-being. Internals are seen as more effective in the workplace, specifically in terms of leadership, management, and decision-making. They tend to be better problem solvers and take ownership and responsibility for decisions. Internals also report less overall workplace anxiety and stress as compared to externals, and they demonstrate a greater level of perseverance and resilience, especially in the face of challenges and adversity.

Studies looking at overall wealth accumulation and income levels show a strong correlation between prosperity and having an internal locus of control. In his book, *Chance or Choice,* Stephen Nowicki discusses the impact of a CEO's locus of control on the financial performance of a company. Companies led by an internal leader performed better financially than those companies led by an external leader.

As I continued my research and worked with leaders and entrepreneurs, it became clear that having an internal locus of control correlated to better overall work and life satisfaction. Internals seemed better able to navigate situational ambiguity and respond more positively to changing and evolving environments.

The following table summarizes the main characteristics associated with both an internal and external locus of control. There's little question that having a strong internal locus of control correlates to better overall results in our lives.

Internal Locus of Control

- Belief in control over one's life
- Improved ability to learn new information
- Better decision-making
- Self-efficacy
- Better job effectiveness
- Higher achievement
- Better overall financial outlook
- Greater happiness
- Increased leadership ability
- Better overall health and well-being

External Locus of Control

- Belief that life is not in one's control
- Success and failure are perceived as a product of luck or chance
- Tendency to blame others/environment
- Easily overwhelmed with tasks
- Sees little value in learning new information
- Lower overall job satisfaction
- Lower overall life happiness
- Higher reported physical symptoms
- Self-defeating thought patterns

Figure 1.1 Key characteristics of internals and externals.

IDENTIFYING YOUR LOCUS OF CONTROL ORIENTATION

Now, at this point, you may be wondering what your locus of control orientation is.

There are a few ways you can find out. First, you can search online for Julian Rotter's Locus of Control Scale and how to access it. It may take you to a journal or publication page, or you may find other resources that include his inventory.

There is, however, a second instrument you can use, that I prefer and recommend, which is Patricia Duttweiler's Internal Control Index. This index consists of a self-report inventory of 28 items and a scoring rubric. Duttweiler's inventory is good for measuring the degree to which a person identifies with an internal locus of control. This is particularly helpful because it provides a more granular understanding of our place along the continuum rather than a more binary representation.

I have secured permission to include Duttweiler's inventory and scoring rubric, and you can find a copy at the back of this book. For those listening to the audiobook, there is an audio section included to help you walk through this inventory.

If you find your score to be more external on Rotter's assessment, or lower on Duttweiler's Internal Control Index, you may wonder if and how it's possible to become more of an internal.

Through all my research around locus of control, I found plenty of information suggesting correlations and associations with either positive or negative life outcomes. Yet there's little research and guidance out there on *how* we form our locus of control orientation, *when* it's formed, and *how we can change it* so we can develop and strengthen an internal locus of control.

It's interesting to note that Nowicki mentions an internal locus of control can be more common in firstborn children. This statement got me thinking. What if that's not by accident?

What if it has to do with the way firstborn children learn and grow in the world? What if locus of control can be learned—and perhaps unlearned? What if our locus of control can be changed?

In a study of hundreds of twin pairs, Susan Bullers and Carol Prescott evaluated what the most significant factors were that determined locus of control orientation. They found that the majority of factors that influenced the twins' perceived locus of control were not due to inherited, psychosocial factors.

While locus of control was previously thought to be a stable trait over time, research on neuroplasticity and cognitive neuroscience reveals we can change or strengthen our locus of control. It's also possible for us to score as an overall internal along the locus of control continuum and, at the same time, operate from a more external locus when it comes to certain areas in our lives. This dichotomy highlights a crucial point about locus of control. While we may *know* we have more control over our lives, we may also, at the same time, *feel* we aren't in control.

This was the case with me. I was more internal on both Rotter's and Duttweiler's inventories, yet I found myself stuck repeating patterns in some areas of my life that felt completely outside of my control. In those areas, I was operating like an external. On some level, I had this knowledge that I was more in control than not, yet I didn't know how stop repeating the negative patterns.

PATTERNS OF BEHAVIOR DURING ADVERSITY

During the housing crisis that began in 2008, I was working with an attorney whose practice included estate planning, business, and real estate law. Seeing what was happening in our community, and to some of our clients and their friends and families, we cofounded a nonprofit legal agency to support people, pro bono, who were struggling to keep their homes.

Our vision was to help them work with their lenders, stay in their homes, and weather the economic downturn so they could achieve greater financial stability. We felt it was important to provide this at no charge because we saw opportunistic pop-up companies forming and pursuing homeowners behind in their payments. They would agree to negotiate on their behalf with the mortgage companies, and then take a fee for time and money saved.

While this approach may have helped some folks in the short-term, we talked with many clients who were frustrated that they had believed such marketing promises and paid money to see little, if any, results. We wanted to be different. We believed there would be a direct and positive benefit to our communities and our businesses if we could stabilize homeownership in our areas. And yet, banks were resistant to accepting loan modifications and slow on approving short sales.

It was during this work that I noticed some interesting patterns with our clients. While they sought help because they were behind on loan payments and worried about losing their homes, their mortgage wasn't the underlying issue. In fact, as we worked with them, we realized that the real crux of the problem, and ultimately what would determine their future outcome, was in how they perceived their predicament.

Specifically, there were two very different belief systems our clients held that influenced how they saw their situations. First, there were the clients who came to us upset that this was happening to them. Those were often their exact words. "We can't believe this is happening to us." They wanted to find loopholes allowing them to get out of their mortgage contracts, which they felt were now unfair because their home values had plummeted. These clients showed little willingness to take any responsibility for how their own decisions may have brought about or contributed to their current situation.

Granted, banks had been approving large loans for borrowers around 2005. Some had adjustable rates that were increasing right when the housing crisis was at its height. So, there's no question there was plenty of responsibility to go around. Yet, when we asked our clients why they had borrowed so much money when they had many other expenses, or why they didn't choose a more affordable home, many said, "Because the bank told me I could afford this."

Another client showed me her cell phone bill. She had five people on her plan. She insisted that she needed to pay for her adult son, his girlfriend, and her sister because they "fell on tough times" and couldn't afford their own phone plans. This client was four months behind on her mortgage, and her home had just been scheduled for auction.

Another couple refused to give up a timeshare in Florida because they had invested so much time in it and had reached a high-status level of "ownership." When I asked them if they could change the locks on this timeshare property, they looked at me surprised and said, "Well, of course not!" I then gently reminded them that they didn't really own it. They were simply paying for scheduled access.

Despite all of this, we did our best to help these clients. At times, we were able to make a difference and help them reduce many of their discretionary expenses. This provided them some relief, even though many did not seem particularly grateful. They tended to get somewhat preachy. For example, one couple lectured me on the ills of banks and how the politicians and those on Wall Street had caused these problems and that they were their hapless victims. They were unwilling to take responsibility for their own financial decisions. There was always someone or something external to blame.

The second type of belief system we noticed was in the clients who came to us readily acknowledging that they had a problem. They saw their financial situation for what it was. And, while not happy with it, they knew they needed to cut their spending and change how they managed money. They took responsibility for adjusting their lifestyles and their expectations. And they were accepting of the possibility that they may need to give up their home, find a place to rent, and work to stabilize their finances. Many even admitted they were financially stretched before the recession and knew that this would eventually catch up with them. They found the process tough, yet many were grateful for our help and the opportunity to make sound changes. These clients were open to options and to finding new opportunities. Some switched careers because they had lost their current jobs. Others started their own companies and became successful business owners and entrepreneurs. Some even moved out of state to completely start over. In the years that followed, I heard from a few of them who said it was because of the lessons they learned from their adversities in 2008 and 2009 that they were now thriving.

What was the difference between these two sets of clients?

It wasn't their level of financial hardship, as many had equal levels of debt and were equally underwater in their repayment of their mortgages. It had to do with the degree to which they felt responsible for their lives and the extent to which they believed that they had the ability to take greater control and change it. Specifically, it was their locus of control orientation.

Those who believed they were ultimately responsible for taking charge of their lives, making changes and different decisions, and adjusting their behavior, fared much better in the short and long run. Those who blamed poor timing, circumstances, and "powerful" others (lenders, politicians, investors) fared much worse and continued to struggle years later. None of these clients had complete control over every aspect that touched their lives, but those who had a stronger belief in their own agency were able to take the reins, and this made an enormous difference to the outcomes they experienced.

PATTERNS OF BEHAVIOR IN ENTREPRENEURS

In the past ten years, I've had the privilege of teaching entrepreneurship to undergraduate and graduate students and working with more than a hundred entrepreneurs in various industries. This has offered me a unique vantage point to observe another interesting pattern.

Originally, my teaching and mentoring approach was practical and process oriented. We would complete a business plan, talk through the financial components, and then work to select and incorporate the appropriate legal entity. For example, we'd decide whether to choose an LLC, a partnership, or some other business arrangement. At this point, I saw so much excitement in the eyes of these budding entrepreneurs. They had such motivation and momentum as they chose their business name and filed the appropriate paperwork. They would order business cards, set up a website, and excitedly tell their friends and family that they had started a business! Some of them launched quickly and made impressive amounts of money in the first few months. One launched an online retail business selling apparel and looked to be well on the way to profit and scaling up. Another began selling dropship products like planners, journals, and organizers.

Yet, once they had secured a few paying clients and had brought in some good income, I noticed a familiar pattern emerging. Many would pull back, lose interest, get distracted by another business or product (shiny object), or find a reason not to move their business forward.

When I asked why they weren't getting new clients and growing their company, they would always have a reason. "Oh, so I was offered a job at Business X, and I figured that would be good because I have student loans to pay off and I need benefits," or, "Well, I was thinking, maybe I could do this part-time, while I do something else," or, "I think I want to go to grad school and I'm not sure I can balance it with running a business." All rational reasons, for sure. And yet, all of them had the same effect: They didn't move forward with their own business.

Fortunately, I had been studying locus of control when I began working with a business student named Nick who fell into this trap. Nick was about to finish his degree and was starting a small business doing woodworking and design. He was an incredible artisan—detail-oriented and highly skilled—and he took immense pride in his work. Everyone marveled at his well-designed masterpieces. However, Nick struggled to get his business to grow past a certain income. Early on, he thought his only chance for success was to ask another company to hire him to grow a segment of their business.

While he was always working on an order, he knew he needed more clients and more employees to better scale his time. Yet he always seemed to be stuck at a certain point and unable to move forward. And, when he did close a deal, he struggled with how much to charge as he wasn't sure how much his work was really worth. One client even backed out of a project, costing Nick considerable time and money for materials. When we talked about why he didn't obtain a 50% down payment to safeguard against this, he said it was because he didn't feel like he could ask for that up-front. Nick was also concerned about how his business would affect his life. He was planning to get engaged soon and had concerns, not only about money but also about his time. He worried that he couldn't be a successful entrepreneur and still spend enough time with his family.

While it would be easy to point to a myriad of outside factors—the marketplace, the economy, or the nature of being an entrepreneur—Nick was fully in control of the pressure he was feeling and the results he was seeing, or not seeing.

Recognizing this, I took a different approach. We spent our sessions talking about the subconscious mind and trying to figure out what might be holding him back. I asked Nick what beliefs he had around owning a business and being an entrepreneur. He told me that, while he wasn't really aware of any particular beliefs he had, each time he saw his parents, they would ask him, "When are you going to get a real job?" He said, when he was growing up, his family viewed being an entrepreneur as risky and something that people only did when they couldn't get a job.

Beliefs are formed and stored in the subconscious mind. We may not even be consciously aware that we have them. They take root when we are very young and become reinforced through time and experience. Like an automatic program, these thoughts and beliefs had been running below the threshold of Nick's conscious awareness. They were sending his conscious brain prompts that he wasn't good enough, or that his work wasn't worth much, or that he could never be in business for himself and make a good living.

While Nick consciously wanted to operate a successful business, deep down, he didn't believe he could. He would make incremental progress, see some promising results, then subconsciously create a reason for why being an entrepreneur may not work out. It was only when Nick became aware of this tendency that he was able to gain greater control over his business and in his life. He found ways in which to scale his time by hiring a team so the business could grow and expand while he still created space in his life for family and friends.

PUTTING IT ALL TOGETHER

I noticed these patterns showing up in leaders, especially within higher education institutions. My dissertation looked at alternate and innovative higher education models in the twenty-first century. I spoke with the top leadership at several institutions that had innovated new teaching, operating, and funding models to make their institutions massively successful. I wanted to find that secret sauce behind their success, especially during times when questions about the value proposition of higher education abounded.

What I thought would result in a list of creative strategies, ideas, or tactics really came down to the mindsets of these top leaders and, as you may have guessed, how much internal control they believed they had over the institution's success, despite a changing educational landscape. I saw themes and trends in the way these leaders spoke and how they thought about success. Yes, they had implemented new and innovative strategies and initiatives, yet the secret sauce was what they believed and perceived was possible for them and for their institutions.

I was now a few years into my study of locus of control and I had formed a hypothesis as to what might have been happening in the minds of the interviewees who answered my locus question. There were likely two answers fighting to come out. One answer would come up quickly, quietly, and intuitively: that they had full control over their own thoughts and behaviors. However, as soon as that answer came to mind, their rational brain caught it and sought to change it. Perhaps the thought process was this: Wait, that can't be right. If I was that in control of my life, then it wouldn't be so chaotic. I wouldn't be in fights with my partner, or struggling to stay in shape, or fighting back emotional outbursts because my days are so stressful and overwhelming. Surely, if I had more control, then my life wouldn't look or feel like this!

What they were struggling with was accepting that they may have more control over their lives than they thought, and yet, at the same time, there were areas of their lives not as they would want them to be. It was easier (and safer) to believe that the reasons for this were not their own doing. Or, more specifically, that they were not within their ability to control. Yet were they really?

CHAPTER 2

THE SUBCONSCIOUS MIND: THE SEAT OF OUR LOCUS OF CONTROL

I'm going to make a bold assertion: We all have much more control over our lives, whether we believe it or not. We are producing the results we see—or, more accurately, our subconscious is, and in this way, we all actually possess an internal locus. However, often, we may not be aware of how it is operating or how to get control of it, so many of our thoughts, feelings, behaviors, and reactions feel external to us, as if they are happening around us or to us, and so it seems rational to believe that external factors such as other people, events, or circumstances are producing our reality.

And even in situations or circumstances where we may not be fully in control, we can look at how much control we *do* have over our perceptions, actions, and reactions. Now, for my highly analytical readers—whom I love as you help us ask the necessary questions to think critically and evaluate information—I want to be clear. I do not suggest we are in control of every occurrence, situation, or environmental factor around us. Weather, natural disasters, pandemics, accidents, and the like can impact our lives regardless of our intentions.

Regardless of what occurs in our lives, we have complete control over how and what we choose to think, feel, and do in response. We even have control over the psychological mechanism that interprets and perceives an event, and then what we decide it means to us. We control all of this.

THE COMPASS AND THE MAGNET

I'll use a metaphor useful for understanding the true nature of the mind. Imagine it operating like a compass and a magnet. The compass is our conscious mind, the direction and goals we intentionally set for ourselves and our life. The magnet is our subconscious mind. It contains all the memories, learnings, associations, beliefs, and filters that were created in our first decade of life and that remain largely unchanged, unless we take control and change them.

Together, the compass and the magnet determine the direction of our life, and the people and situations that we attract in it. Our magnet mind is the more powerful of the two, however, and when it's in conflict with the direction of the compass, it will alter its trajectory, hold it back, and knock it off course.

Most of the time, when trying to effect change, we focus our efforts solely on our conscious mind, or the thoughts and beliefs we know about and are aware of. We think that's where the power and the ability to change resides. Yet, we find ourselves repeating the same patterns over and over again. This is why it's easy to fall into the external locus of control trap. Despite repeated efforts to change our thoughts, behaviors and results, we feel stuck and believe there must be more powerful people or forces blocking our forward progress.

And yet, in reality, it's our subconscious, magnet mind that is in control of our thoughts and actions and not our conscious, compass mind. Our subconscious mind attracts or repels people, situations, or events depending on the information it's gathered and stored inside it over time. It accepts that information that aligns with what it knows and has known, and repels that which doesn't align or match what it has known, regardless if this is good or useful for us or not. This is why we may recall hearing variations on the saying that we don't attract what we want but what we are. This magnet mind is affected by the belief systems (inputs) that have been inside of it for years. This is similar to a concept called hysteresis that happens with magnetic materials. It refers to the way a system is influenced by its history so that there's a lag between when we input new information into it (for example, to change the direction of the magnet) and when it responds (the movement of the magnet). The key is knowing how this works so you can get it working for you.

In a 2005 article in *US News & World Report*, Marianne Szegedy-Maszak explained that most of our decisions, behaviors, and actions are driven by the 95% of the brain that operates outside of conscious awareness—our subconscious. At first, this percentage can seem staggering, especially because it may challenge our understanding of what conscious and subconscious mean. For example, I had no idea that my subconscious mind was at work all the time, day and night. I thought it was only active when I fell asleep. I didn't know that the subconscious mind operated in such an automatic and associative fashion.

But this is exactly how our brain is designed to operate. It automates that which we repeatedly do. It off-loads decisions, associations, thought patterns, and reactions from the conscious system to the more autonomic, subconscious processing system. Neuroimaging points to the neural basis for how decision-making is driven by emotions, impulses, and autonomic processes operating below the threshold of our conscious awareness. It feels out of our control, yet it's very much *within* our control and it's pulling the proverbial strings.

A good illustration of this is the backwards bike. If you search on Google or YouTube for *backwards bike*, you will see a video documenting an experiment some engineers undertook using a regular, two-wheel bicycle. They changed the orientation of the handlebars so that when you turn the handle left, the bike wheel points right, and when you turn the handle right, the wheel moves to the left. The engineers took the bike to speaking events all over the world, offering people money to try to ride the bike on stage. They explained the bike's reverse orientation beforehand, so the volunteers were prepared. The results were fascinating, though not surprising. Even though people knew the bike was made this way, they were unable to successfully ride it. Each time, you would see someone say, "Sure, I can do this." Then, after a few seconds, they realized they could not even ride it a few feet.

The narrator explains that riding a bike is an ideomotor activity, meaning it's deeply ingrained in our autonomic nervous system. Even though we know it is "backwards," we cannot ride it until we rewire the neural pathways deeply ingrained in mind and body that enable us to ride a bike. It takes an adult several weeks of continuous practice to learn how to ride the backwards bike, yet a young child can learn in a much shorter time period. This is because, as a child, our brains are much more neuroplastic, meaning that the neurons in our brain can wire (learn) and rewire (relearn) at much faster rates.

As adults, we can still unlearn and relearn, it just takes more time and practice. And it takes an understanding of how our brains work. We must grasp that, while we may know something consciously, until we change the subconscious programming and the corresponding neural pathways that are producing a result, we won't see lasting change.

STUCK IN THE MAGNET MIND

This was exactly what was happening in my own life. I knew the outcomes I saw were the result of my own choices, decisions, and belief systems. And yet, I had no idea how to go inside of myself to make the changes I wanted to. At first, I thought I had an issue with willpower and that I just needed to build more of it. Yet, if you've ever tried relying solely on your will to drive a new exercise routine or healthy eating regime forward, you may have found that this just doesn't work long-term. When we are tired and hungry, affectionately known now by the popular term "hangry," our willpower is at its weakest. It's when we are most susceptible to falling away from a new routine or eating an entire sleeve of Thin Mints Girl Scout cookies—which I've done. More than once.

It's also when we tend to snap at people, become frustrated with situations, and make rash, ill-advised business and personal decisions. Our willpower is more a function of our conscious mind trying to override more autonomic, subconscious drives. It may work for a little while, yet it's not the key to deep change. Our locus of control is not determined by the amount of willpower we have, but on how we work with our more powerful operating system: our magnet mind.

Many of us are moving around the world unaware of what patterns we have stored in our magnet minds and how these control the outcomes in our lives. I know this was true for me. I consciously knew the personal and professional goals that I wanted, yet I didn't recognize the subconscious beliefs I held that were making these goals nearly impossible to attain. These subconscious beliefs are formed when we are very young. They are well-worn neural pathways that have been there a long time. At their very core, however, they have a positive intention: to keep us alive, safe, and able to avoid the pain of loss, disappointment, and abandonment. After all, when we were very young, these were critical to our very survival.

It doesn't seem logical to us as adults that we could be repeating patterns from a place of preserving safety, survival, and our own acceptance (i.e., avoiding abandonment). This is because the logical part of our brains formed much later, long after these fears provoked the protective patterns that took root in our more autonomic subconscious mind. And so, as adults, when we find ourselves in the same painful conversation, job, emotion, or outcome, it is likely the result of these protective magnet mind patterns at work, running below the threshold of our conscious awareness.

So, how do we know if we have these subconscious beliefs sabotaging our thinking and our lives? Like the crew on the starship *Enterprise*, we look for patterns that keep repeating. Clues to the rhythms of our subconscious, magnet mind.

Toward the end of 2009, my marriage was in trouble. Familiar fears, thought patterns, and beliefs were in full swing, and my husband and I were talking divorce, annulment, and dividing the finances. We'd been married for about two-and-a-half years. Fortunately, he suggested counseling. I resisted at first because I remembered beliefs my family had about therapy, psychology in general, and the idea of couples counseling. I had concluded that, if we were even thinking about it, it was probably already over. That was a perfect example of an old (and non-useful) belief. Now, I will say, the counseling journey was a rough one and, many times, we'd leave these sessions feeling worse than when we arrived. I'd come to expect that as normal and figured it had to be difficult for it to produce a positive outcome.

I was probably half-right. It was difficult, but not for the reasons I had thought. It was difficult because both of us were learning how deeply ingrained our old beliefs and behavioral patterns were and, in many cases, we were becoming aware, for the first time, that we even had them. These sessions were not about disagreements over a neat or messy house, taking out the trash, or how to squeeze a tube of toothpaste. They cut to the very core of who we were as human beings and our fears of abandonment, being loved, and feeling worthy.

Of course, neither of us articulated this for years. We would get upset when the other person didn't act or react in the exact way we expected, and we blamed each other for how we felt in the moment. I was convinced we were simply mismatched and remembered my dad once saying, "Relationships are like pots and pot covers. Every pot has a cover, and sometimes the cover doesn't fit the pot." These words carried the power of my dad's voice. Ever since I was a young girl, my dad had authority in my world. This is true of most parent/child relationships.

A few years (yes, years) into therapy, it became clear that, while we were both committed to the relationship and we had made some incremental improvements, things had not really changed all that much. There were small steps, here or there, but I noticed I was slipping back into old, familiar thought patterns. Is this right for me? What if I'm not happy enough? Why doesn't our relationship look more like a Hallmark channel love story? Will we make it to 10 years? Does he really love me? Would I be better off if I ran away now? And those were the positive thoughts.

I became very frustrated. I had had enough of talking and trying to figure out what wasn't working. I wanted solutions.

I wanted real and lasting change. While I didn't have the slightest idea how to get it, somehow, I had this knowledge inside of me that real and positive change was possible and that we'd be healthier and happier on the other side of it. Yet, we were not on the other side of it in that moment. Therapy was starting to feel like an old record stuck on a turntable. It was like the same day replaying over and over again—like on the *Enterprise*.

And, just like on the *Enterprise*, I was trying to figure out how to stop the pattern. I was searching for how to gain more control over the root cause so I could change it. I remember feeling like I was on this deep-dive journey. A journey to the center of myself. I was recognizing behavior patterns that had been repeating for years.

Like the record on the turntable, the facts and people may have been different, yet the tune was familiar, and the outcome was the same. There was one common denominator, one constant variable. Me.

IDENTITY VERSUS BEHAVIOR

Before we can gain more control over our lives, we have to first be willing to disidentify with much of who and what we think is us. What we think is our identity may be holding us back by limiting what we believe we can be. I know this was true for me. I had to understand that my identity as a person was separate from my behavior, whether this presented as thoughts, emotions, feelings, past experiences, or mistakes. I realized that I needed to change myself and my thoughts before I could even think about changing anything else, including my relationship. I needed to figure out what parts of me were my identity, and what parts were my behaviors or behavioral patterns that I *could* change.

For years, I had thought of my identity and my behavior as pretty much the same thing. I was outgoing, energetic, an extrovert, talkative, an external processor, deeply emotional, a bit anxious, and extremely sensitive. This felt like the essence of who I was and I had become attached to it; the familiarity of my behavior became reassuring.

Indeed, we can become defensive if this strong connection to our identity (aka self-worth) is threatened. If someone challenges us on an "I am" statement, we tend to become protective, as if they are attacking an arm or a leg. Our subconscious mind wants us to be happy, but if it has to choose between keeping us safe and keeping us happy, it will choose safety every time. This means protecting and repeating familiar behaviors, even if they aren't healthy or useful today.

The value in this realization—that we are not our behavior—is that positive change is possible. Our identity may feel fixed and immutable, but our behavior can always be modified. And we can change our beliefs and behaviors without changing the essence of who we are. Our behaviors are merely learned neural pathways in our brain, like riding a bike—decisions we made time and time again. The more a neuron fires, the stronger it becomes, and the easier and more rapidly it will refire in the future.

As we saw with the backwards bike, our brains are neuroplastic, meaning they can change and adapt in response to new and different experiences, even if this is harder as we get older. The old saying, "Well that's just how I'm wired," may not be entirely correct. It may be how we are currently wired, yet new experiences and conscious choices to think or act differently can rewire (and refire) our brains.

In his book, *Personality Isn't Permanent*, Benjamin Hardy explains that it is our experiences, especially our early ones, that shape our personality. As such, our personality is not immutable. New experiences can reshape and change it.

DISIDENTIFYING FROM YOUR BEHAVIORS

To build a strong internal locus of control, we must embrace this journey to the center of ourselves, resist the temptation to identify with non-useful beliefs, behaviors and thought patterns, and change whatever is necessary for us to see a better outcome. We have to be willing to let go of what is not working.

As we've seen, we hold close the things that we identify with, as if they are extensions of us. This makes it harder for us to change them. Yet, if we can separate ourselves from them and see them as patterns over which we have control, then we can realize lasting positive change. We are more than our mistakes, more than our memories, and more than the repeated patterns we've struggled with in our lives.

This is also why language is so important. When we use "I" statements like, "I am a doctor," or, "I am a lawyer," or, "I am a scientist," what we do for a living becomes part of who we are. This can be useful until it's not. If we lose our job, or want to change jobs, or just want to be valued for who we are rather than what we do, it no longer supports our development. Yet, if we can use language like, "I currently practice medicine," or, "I work as a research scientist for …," then we can feel some sense of separation between what we do and who we are.

The same can be said for when we make statements like, "I am an anxious person," or, "That's just me, anxiety-city!" Imagine if I said, "Up until now, I've done anxiety all too well," or, "I am working to change my anxiety patterns." Could a subtle yet powerful distinction like that transform my locus of control?

I recognize this is much easier said than done. It can be professionally and personally devastating to lose a job or stop working in a certain profession. During the recession, I saw this firsthand. Clients who had strongly identified with their work and who lost their jobs faced more significant challenges with their physical and mental health.

But what we identify with exerts power over us. It controls our emotions, feelings, beliefs, actions, and reactions. It controls how we see ourselves and what we believe about the world. And yet, the good news in all of this is that, ultimately, we do have control over what we identify with. And we can use this to align ourselves more closely with how we *want* to think and feel, and distance ourselves from what we don't. We can decide what we want to identify with and what we want closely connected to us in way that makes our lives better. And, in doing this, we will see and feel better results in our lives.

Here's a helpful activity to help you better define and delineate between identity and behavior. Write down five positive statements about yourself that you want to identify with. In essence, select aspects you *want* to link to your identity. For example:

- I am compassionate.
- I am generous.
- I am loving.
- I am valued.

Notice how you immediately feel a sense of calm and ease. Now, write down five statements that explain what you don't like about yourself and word them in ways that allow you to state you are changing them. For example:

- "At times, I react poorly to stressful situations. I'm working on improving this, because I am safe and loved."

- "At times, I react with frustration or impatience. I'm aware of this and working to change it. I am compassionate and generous."

It's important to include the second part of the statement that makes it clear you are aware of your issue and that you are working to change it. It gives your brain the coordinates to head toward, as well as the awareness that these are simply behaviors. While they may be familiar, they are not permanent, and they can change.

CHAPTER 3

THE POWER OF EARLY EXPERIENCES I: PERCEPTION VERSUS REALITY

THE TETHERED ELEPHANT: LIMITING BELIEFS
There's a well-known story about how a baby elephant learns not to escape from its keeper. When the elephant is very young, it is tied to a tree or post with a chain around one of its legs. The chain is strong enough to keep the baby elephant from breaking away, so it learns to stay within the range the chain permits.

As the elephant grows up and gets stronger, the keeper replaces the chain with a much weaker rope. The elephant still doesn't wander away or attempt to break free. It remembers the feeling of being tethered as a baby elephant. Even though it has become an adult, and the simple rope and post would be easy for it to break away from, it still believes it cannot escape.

Just as the adult elephant still holds beliefs it formed long ago from its early experiences, so too do we hold onto old beliefs from our own early experiences. And, like the belief that the rope was a barrier to its freedom, our old beliefs can be barriers to our own.

As with the elephant, if we repeatedly act in response to these beliefs, they can become ingrained in our neurology.

We procrastinate because we are afraid of moving forward on a project, taking a new job, or starting a new venture. Our mind learns to etch that act of procrastination deeply into our neural pathway. This keeps us "safe," because we've learned that moving forward may lead to failure, and at the same time, like the elephant and the rope, it holds us back. Yet it does not need to be this way.

Years ago, it was thought that the brain didn't and couldn't change much when we grew older. Hence the popular phrase, "You can't teach an old dog new tricks." And, although our brains are more receptive to change when we're young, neuroscience has shown, especially in the last decade, that our brains are incredibly neuroplastic and can change in response to a myriad of new experiences, especially those we have as adults. Evidence of our brain's ability to rewire can be seen in stroke victims or those who have suffered brain damage and then recover some or all of their prior functioning. It's not because the damaged tissue repaired itself, but rather that the brain learns how to rewire functions and processes around that damaged tissue. In essence, it adapts.

This works for our locus of control as well. Just because we may identify with a more external locus at some point in our lives or in some areas, doesn't mean we have to stay this way. We can rewire and strengthen our internal locus of control. Of course, this feels uncomfortable at first. It can feel very unfamiliar, like we are a fish out of water. It is only when we begin to change our deeply held beliefs and perceptions that we will see real change in our lives.

TWO LENSES: CREATING OUR OWN REALITY

Our brains have evolved to keep us alive and safely moving through the world. And as we move through the world, information is passed through our perceptual filters, or our five senses. That is our inner lens, yet it's shaped by our brain's expectations and predictions. We see what we believe we will see based upon our past experiences. These experiences impact how information is filtered and taken in. This is both for the brain to operate efficiently and also to establish predictability, two outcomes it is constantly striving to attain. And, there are times this is useful. For example, we may get a sixth sense that walking down a certain street may be dangerous based on our experiences and accumulated knowledge in the past. On the other hand, there are times when this filter can become a bias, either confirming what we want to see despite objective evidence to the contrary, or assuming a situation or event will turn out a certain way because of a prior experience when, in reality, we have incredible control to change it for the better. We are not bound by our past, any more than we are set in any certain future.

Imagine for a moment that there are two lenses through which we see the world. One lens is the way the world actually is. It is independent of any filter, judgment, or perspective. Then, there is a second lens. This lens is shaped by our past experiences and our conscious and subconscious beliefs about the way the world should be. It is activated almost instantly when experiencing the world and, if we don't understand how this works, it can feel like it's the first lens—that it is reality itself. And yet, it is not. It is our interpretation of reality, our perception. If we do nothing to check or audit this second lens, it will always adjust the reality to align with our beliefs, perceptions, and subconscious associations. We will see the world as we *expect* it to be.

This inner lens through which we filter reality also impacts the perceptual filters through which we take in information: our five senses. Data from the world comes into our minds through these: sight, sound, taste, touch, and smell. Because there is so much information around us in the world at any given time, our senses can only process a small fraction of it. In order to sort for what's most important to us, information gets deleted, distorted, or generalized. And the litmus test for how this information is processed is shaped by that second lens—our belief and perception lens. We can literally delete information we see, hear, taste, touch, or smell if this information does not match our inner beliefs. As such, we create our own reality.

This is how our mind can hold us back and stall change. For years, my perceptions around relationships and love were distorted and skewed by my own belief systems. I filtered for certain characteristics in other people that were familiar, even though they were not healthy. And our brains will choose familiar over healthy, because familiar is associated with being safe. The brain figures that because it has kept us alive up until now, what it has done before has worked, and thus it tends toward repeating those familiar patterns. But what has helped us survive may not be what is needed to help us thrive.

In my own life, I had a set of deeply ingrained beliefs that shaped the way I thought romantic relationships should be. These beliefs had come from childhood fairy tales, Hallmark movies, and attachment associations to early influential figures. These early experiences and associations have tremendous impact on our adult selves and who we *feel* attracted to. We may not be aware that often we are attracted to people who subconsciously match those familiar experiences and remind us of the people from whom we sought acceptance when we were young.

For example, sometimes, it's a relationship with someone early on in our lives (perhaps a parent, sibling, or relative) that we wanted to like us and give us attention. Sometimes, it's an association from our past that our brain encoded as positive, loving, or intriguing. We may not even remember or be fully aware of this connection. We simply sense that something about a person we meet today feels "right" and attracts us. It's often less about the actual person and more about how we *feel* about that person that drives initial attraction and attachment.

At first, I resisted this notion. I thought of all the times we hear about people who end up with someone so unlike anyone in their lives. The teenager who dates someone completely different from their father or mother, or even themselves— the proverbial opposites attract. Deep down, though, there's something about that connection, that relationship, that is familiar to them.

Most of us have some remnants from our childhood of old, less-than-useful relationship associations. Even in the healthiest of familial homes, there will be times when we are hypervigilant children, observing every look or grimace from a parent or caregiver, and then forming a conclusion about what this means about us or to us. This is simple survival. We are trying to figure out what pleases people and what doesn't, and we are constantly searching for signs we are loved and valued. And we are also watching how our parents relate to each other, or to those who are important in their lives. How they show love, affection, and attention. We hear words like *love*, and we then associate this with all kinds of behavior that we observe. The more it occurs, the stronger the association gets, especially during our first seven years of life. After that time, unless we become aware of how powerful this initial encoding can be, our subconscious mind has locked these automatic associations away for future use.

All of this drops unfiltered into our magnet mind. And when we start dating or entering into adult relationships, these patterns get activated. For example, if we had an insecure attachment or difficult relationship with a primary caregiver, even though on the surface the caregiver may appear to be doting and protective, the feeling inside generated by that relationship is one of tentativeness, insecurity, and uncertainty. Those feelings become familiar to us and associated with love. We then subconsciously seek out relationships and people that ping on this familiar pattern, and the cycle continues.

Have you ever known someone who seems to date the same type of person over and over, even when it's clearly not doing them any good? They might assure you, with each new partner, "This time will be different," or, "They are so much better than so-and-so," but they are essentially in the same relationship. This pattern keeps repeating, begging to be broken, like Groundhog Day. Ask them if they feel in control over their feelings and the likely answer will be no. Their reality is entirely driven by their unhealthy perception of what love feels like, and they will often have no idea how to take back the reins and change their behavior.

This split between perception and reality doesn't just play out in relationship dramas; it shows up in every area of our lives. For years, I believed that, once people got to know me, they would hurt me, dislike me, abandon me, or hate me. I believed this because I had early childhood experiences of friends teasing, bullying, and excluding me. Some were so horrible it took me until my late thirties to be able to talk about them without crying or getting physically upset. My brain desperately tried to figure out what happened so it could prevent this type of pain in the future. In response, it formed a belief upon which my reality was based. On a subconscious level, I feared being all alone in the world with no friends, no family, and no one to love me. Of course, no amount of rational thought or statements like, "Oh that's ridiculous, you are wonderful," or, "That's not true, it's not you," would help because the belief is encoded deeply in the subconscious mind.

Our brains create a loop, a pattern, to prevent the pain. This pattern would either compel me not to form close friendships, or when I did, if there was a disagreement or a conflict, I would automatically think that this meant the person would hate me and the friendship would be over. The same thing happened in my romantic relationships and then, years later, in my marriage.

Deep down, I believed something was fundamentally wrong with me. These accumulated experiences from childhood—feeling ostracized, teased, excluded—had shaped me. A young person's mind doesn't have the knowledge or perspective to understand these situations for what they are: children being mean, which is a part of life. It was hard to accept that they didn't happen because of something I did or who I was. My mind thus formed the belief that this would not have happened if I was more likable, or more attractive, or smarter, or [fill in the blank].

This non-useful or, as many psychologists and counselors call it, limiting belief, influenced my perception of people and relationships for years. When my husband and I had a disagreement, or when I perceived him acting in ways that didn't match my concept of love or appreciation, I concluded that he no longer loved me and the marriage was doomed. Of course, then I acted in ways that perpetuated this "reality" and hence the pattern continued.

Talking with friends and colleagues through the years, I realized I wasn't alone. This is a common pattern in relationships. As human beings, we are seeking validation, love, and affirmation. And we have a preset belief or blueprint of what that looks like and what behavior and words are needed to give us that. Many times, when the other person doesn't do or say what we are looking for, we conclude that must mean: They don't love me, care for me, or want me.

All of this happens deep in our subconscious mind, beyond the threshold of our conscious awareness. What happens consciously are fights over time spent away, the house being left a mess, or someone not calling. People will argue for years about these things when the genuine issues are much deeper and quite simple. We create our own reality, perpetuate the same script, and we repeat the same argument, even though we don't *consciously* want to. And, all of this feels like it's out of our control.

Finally, similar beliefs and behaviors happen in our career and professional life too. When I was in kindergarten, my teacher got upset at me for getting a plastic egg stuck in a cup that was too small for it. I likely wanted to put the egg in there and, when it didn't fit easily, I forced it in, so it stuck. The entire incident was quite unsettling, as the teacher got terribly upset, called my mom, and accused me of doing it on purpose or being stupid enough not to know it wouldn't fit.

Now, you would think something this ridiculous, and it sounds even more ridiculous as I write it, would never impact me in my twenties and thirties. And maybe this incident alone didn't, yet it made such an impression that my brain made a note of it. I was five, so in a highly impressionable time period of life, and this was an authority figure, my teacher.

Fast-forward a few years, and I was struggling with a speech impediment in the second grade. I said my r's as w's and my t's as k's, so words like rabbit and kitty came out wabbit and, well, you get the picture. It was so bad that my teacher recommended I be put in a remedial speech course or get speech therapy. My dad was concerned about putting me in a remedial class, so he worked with me every day on the drive to and from school. I never needed that speech class, yet I never forgot that I almost did.

Through grade and high school, I earned good grades, though never scored off the charts on the SATs or ACTs. My mom would often say that I was good at reading and creative writing, yet I wasn't really a math or science person. I spent my four years at the University of Michigan convinced I never should have gotten in. I remember joking that they admitted me by mistake because I was nowhere near as smart as some of my high school friends who had not been accepted. All of this takes a toll on your self-confidence, and I don't share it to opine about my past, but to make a point about how my early experiences, and the belief systems they forged, shaped my reality, even though it was not the objective reality of the situation.

Three graduate degrees later, and I found myself still struggling with my self-worth.

Can you see how this plays out? It was one of those never-ending loops, and it would have repeated unless I noticed what was happening and changed it. The truth was, it wasn't out of my control; in fact, I was (subconsciously) controlling it. I just didn't realize it.

This is what has often been called a self-fulfilling prophecy. We expect something to happen on a subconscious level and have primed our perceptual filters to recognize and even to sort for what is in harmony with this expectation. We tend to dismiss and delete things not congruent with those magnet-mind expectations.

Here's an example. If we believe we are not smart enough to earn a promotion, or be hired into a leadership position, we will subconsciously find ways to sabotage possible new opportunities. We'll blame those in positions of leadership for not recognizing our hard work and constantly point out what they are not doing well. We will refrain from looking for or applying for leadership roles because we tell ourselves we don't want that kind of stress and responsibility, or that we don't want to be seen as part of the upper management folks. And our behavior at work and in meetings with colleagues will subtly reflect these inner beliefs. The energy we bring into the room, the way we interact and speak about others, and the way we view the world all factor into the way we show up and the opportunities that come our way—or not.

That will be what our magnet mind attracts and brings into our lives. We are fulfilling the expectations we have for ourselves. Our reality is based on our perception of it, and that perception is influenced by our internal belief systems about ourselves and the world. It is, effectively, biased.

ACTIVITY: RECOGNIZING OUR PATTERNS OF PERCEPTION

Here's an activity that can help you shift the way you perceive reality. Notice a pattern of thought that appears often. It may show up at work, with your family, or in your primary relationship. It is usually based on a fear that something will happen to us. Either someone will do something to you or a situation will happen that will cause you great distress.

Instead of focusing on what you may think is causing this in the environment around you, identify what the underlying belief is that you have about yourself or the world that is the trigger. Ask yourself what your earliest memory is related to when you formed that belief or conclusion. Most of the time, this will be when you were very young. It will involve family or close friends, and it will relate to an event that was painful.

Because of the power of these memories, our minds can kick into overdrive and begin sorting certain types of situations through those perceptual filters, looking for similarities. We are on high alert for danger. Later in this book, I will talk about how we can begin to shift to different and more useful thought patterns. For now, simply becoming aware of this pattern will empower you to see the difference between the reality of a situation and your perception of it. The reality we perceive is filtered through our beliefs about ourselves and the world. Change those beliefs to more useful and productive ones, and we will create a more positive reality for ourselves.

CHAPTER 4

THE POWER OF EARLY EXPERIENCES II: OUR SURVIVAL INSTINCT

Now that we know the impact that childhood attachments have on our adult selves, let's explore why those early, key relationships have so much power over us and how they shape our magnet mind.

OUR PRIMAL AND EMOTIONAL BRAINS

When we're very young, we are focused on survival. Our parent(s) are our primary caregivers. We need them to survive, and we need their love and approval to feel assured that we are safe and will survive. If Mom, Dad, or a sibling is upset with us, then our younger self worries about what this means: Do they love me? If they don't, will they leave me? If they leave me, will I be able to survive on my own? Are they displeased with me? Am I not enough? And if they are displeased with me, and I'm not enough, would they abandon me? And, if they abandoned me, how will I survive? These are the subconscious thoughts that run through our minds at an early age and mold our responses to later experiences. The power of this desire for survival is hard to underestimate. Even if a particular relationship is harmful, if we feel dependent on someone and believe them to have great control and influence over our lives, we will feel a desire to love them and ensure they love us.

You may be aware of Stockholm syndrome? This is where some people form attachment bonds with their kidnappers even if they are abused by them. This is caused by a stress response. In one example, former bank hostages bonded with their captors, and went on to defend them later in court, even offering to pay their legal fees. In some ways, the person forms these bonds as a way to cope with the stress and fear of the situation. To a certain extent, the emotional drivers behind Stockholm syndrome can produce similar results in interpersonal or family relationships. If this seems a bit irrational, it is because it is. It's more emotional, and it taps right into our fears around safety and survival.

As young children, we interpret words, facial expressions, and certain patterns of behavior as indicators of love, approval, acceptance, and worthiness. We believe what we are told because that's all we know. Our brains operate like blank slates, downloading information from the world around us and accepting it as truth. During these formative years, we know, at an instinctual level, that being loved and valued equates to survival; not just physically, but also financially, emotionally, and so on. So, we carry these beliefs forward as we grow up and begin to interact in an adult world.

This instinct for survival is driven by what some people have termed our primal reptile or lizard brain. While not a popular term in contemporary neuroscience, it has been used to refer to the amygdala, or fear center, in our brain that scans our environment for threats to our survival. I started to research this more to learn how it may influence our decisions and maybe even drive our behavior.

In 2009, two trial lawyers, David Ball and Don Keenan, authored the book, *Reptile*.

The book discusses a trial strategy designed to maximize juror awards. The strategy appeals to what is referred to as the reptile part, or amygdala, of a juror's brain to trigger fear, anger, and potentially revenge. The book explains that when jurors are presented with an argument that shows how the plaintiff's injury could have easily happened to them or their loved ones, the plaintiff's attorneys have a better chance of a favorable verdict and higher damage award. The concept is that this reptile part of the brain relies on fear to motivate behavior. There's a telling passage in the book: "I am the reptile, I do not get afraid, I make you afraid so you do what I want. I do not get angry; I make you angry so you will do what I want." While this framework could produce higher awards because it activates the fear center in many a juror's brain, this reptile terminology has been the subject of a lot of debate.

In the 1960s, neuroscientist Paul MacLean put forth his triune brain theory, which made mention of this primal, reptilian brain. This framework proposed the evolution of the brain in three sequential parts. MacLean suggested the most instinctual, fight-or-flight part of the brain formed first (the paleo cortex or basal ganglia), followed by the emotional response part (limbic brain), and then the rational brain (neocortex).

While MacLean's framework may have opened the door to evaluate how the brain responds to certain stimuli, especially in relation to our emotions, contemporary neuroscience and modern brain imaging point to a more integrative model in which emotions are created. They are the complex product of our lived experiences and how our neurons interact in response to learned stimuli. As such, we can change and rewire our responses. Emotions are not inevitable; we have the power to change and reframe them for the better. For example, in *How Emotions Are Made*, Lisa Feldman Barret explains that emotions are constructed in our brains from a lifetime of learned experiences across core systems interacting as a whole.

Because of our powerful survival instinct when we're young, our early emotions and attachments play a significant role, not just in early childhood, but throughout our lives as well. We learn based upon the frameworks and associations we have had in the past. Emotional constructs and reactions are therefore more individualized than we may have previously thought. When we encounter situations in which we do feel loved, safe, accepted, and valued, the fear center of our brain is not active. It has no need to be. We notice positive emotions and responses. We want more of this, and so we tend to seek out that which produces these positive emotions and feelings of safety and security. When we encounter situations where we feel threatened, at risk, unsafe, or unloved, then the emotional part of our brain also lights up and we experience anger, fear, suspicion, distrust, and contempt. We try to avoid these situations.

PATTERN MATCHING AND FINDING A DIFFERENT PATH

We can now see a pattern emerging. We experience an emotion and then take an action in response to that emotion. If positive, we act to experience more of it. If negative, we work to avoid it in the future. Often though, what may feel positive or good *to* us may not be good *for* us. It may simply be that the emotion, the person, the situation, or the event that triggered that emotion is familiar to us. Remember, when given the choice, our brain chooses what is familiar over what may be best for us in the short- and long-term. Our brain focuses on surviving rather than thriving.

In his bestselling book, *Thinking, Fast and Slow*, Daniel Kahneman talks about System 1 and System 2 thinking, which are similar to the subconscious magnet mind and the conscious compass mind. System 1 is the more autonomic, pattern matching, associative mind. It moves quickly, thinks fast, and is quick to form opinions or impressions. System 2 is the more analytical, evaluative mind. It can think through a complex equation or mathematical problem and take the time to balance evidence from various perspectives.

The problem is, we are being driven by System 1 more often than we think. Many times, we believe we are thinking rationally or objectively when assessing a situation. In reality, we are really just pattern patching to prior experiences or emotional responses in our lives. Our brains tend to pick up on change, movement, or that which is out of the norm for our lives and our expectations. Those things that have become normal, or regular, to us are nearly invisible. This is because our brains grow accustomed to them; they become part of our environment and expectation. In essence, we become desensitized by design. Imagine if we heard loud noises every night, or the screaming and arguing of our parents when we were young. Eventually, those sounds become part of our expected reality. We may be aware they are there, yet also not at the same time. And, as we move through the world, situations or circumstances that would seem loud or volatile to some people may not seem out of the norm for others.

This is one of the reasons we tend to repeat patterns in life that produce familiar outcomes even though we consciously want that outcome to be different. We are operating with a dual mind—the conscious compass and the subconscious magnet, driven by the primal and the emotional brains. And when we do venture out and make a conscious choice to think, believe, or behave in a different way, a more useful and healthier way, it feels so unfamiliar to us that our minds put up tremendous resistance. We tell ourselves, this isn't right for me, or this just feels so contrary to who I am.

In his book, *The Coaching Habit: Say Less, Ask More & Change the Way You Lead Forever*, Michael Bungay Stanier likens the poem, "The Road Not Taken," by Robert Frost to the new habit pathways we build for ourselves and our responses when changing old (and well-traveled) behaviors. This is an interesting analogy. Perhaps not only is the process of building new patterns and associations one that involves us using less traveled neural pathways and emotional responses in the brain, but, as Frost said at the end of his poem, taking this road less traveled "made all the difference."

UNDERSTANDING THE SCIENCE: OUR YOUNG BRAINS

We now understand the power our early experiences have over us as adults, but what is the science behind this phenomenon? Why are our young brains so susceptible to outside experiences, and why do they have such a long-lasting impact on our beliefs and behaviors?

When we are very young, our brains are forming and operating from different brain wave states. You may not have heard of brain wave states before, so I'll summarize them here for the purposes of discussing how it is we learn and take in information at different stages of our lives. The important aspect of this to remember is that, just because we are adults now, doesn't mean our subconscious mind isn't still operating programs formed when we were young. In fact, many times throughout our day, we may find ourselves using ways of thinking, processing, and filtering borne of our younger mind.

From birth to age two, our brains function mostly in the lowest brain wave cycles, called delta, which is .5 to four cycles per second. In the delta state, we are functioning primarily from our subconscious mind. We can observe this when we look at small children. I know I see it when I look at my nephew. He is watching what's happening in the outside world, not really able to respond or change it. He sees Mom, Dad, me. All of us feel like extensions of himself. So, if one of us is upset, he feels it as if he is upset.

All of his senses are receiving information about the world and merely accepting what he experiences—whether it's what he sees, hears, smells, tastes, or touches—as absolute truth. Like a computer downloading information directly into its hard drive, young children are downloading all that they experience in their environment directly into their subconscious minds. There is no ability to discern or separate information. Imagine how powerful learning can be in these first two years!

From ages two to six, our brains are operating in the theta state, or between four and eight cycles per second. In the theta state, we spend most of our time imagining and daydreaming. As children, this is when we most often played pretend. Perhaps we imagined we were teaching school or dressing up as our favorite television or cartoon character. We tend to move through the world in a more imaginative state, and we are very receptive to learning new concepts and ideas. This is why we often see children of this age able to learn a new language if the parent or primary caregiver speaks it to them and around them. Their brains are very susceptible to absorption.

Then, from ages six to 12, our brains begin to operate more in the alpha state, or between eight and 13 cycles per second. It's during this time that the analytical mind begins to form, and so the older the child, the more they will operate in the alpha brain wave state. They begin to interpret their experiences and form conclusions about these experiences and interactions. It may still be challenging for them to distinguish reality from fantasy or the world of imagination. This is why we often see parents hesitant to let their kids watch a scary movie or certain content on television. While they can hear us telling them that it's only a movie, their brains still struggle to accept this, which can lead to nightmares or unnecessary anxieties. I'm sure you can remember a time when you saw a scary movie and it haunted you for days, gave you nightmares, and created a fear that what you saw on the screen could happen in your life.

Finally, when we are 12 years of age and older, our brain operates more from the beta state, which is measured at above 13 cycles per second. In this state, we have more capacity for critical and analytical thought. We are more focused, alert, and logical in the way we approach ourselves and the world. Experiences or events we have after age 12, while important, do not have the same power or amplitude within our subconscious programs as those that happened when we were younger. Why? Because when we were younger, we didn't have the ability to keep negative, destructive, or unhealthy thoughts out of our brain. They were readily accepted and formed the foundation of the beliefs and perceptions that we often still have today—even though we may not know we are subconsciously accessing them.

There's an important evolutionary reason for this period of intense enculturation. We must learn thousands upon thousands of facts about how to fit into family and society in order to live our lives. During this time, we are acquiring many important learnings: not to touch a hot stove, or walk too close to a street without holding a grown-up's hand, or talk to strangers who may harm us. If our brains didn't receive these messages so readily and fully, or if we could choose to dismiss them or filter them, then this could impact our ability to survive.

During our early life, therefore, our system is literally designed to make sure that we learn and retain life-saving lessons as quickly as possible. The only problem is that so many other non-useful learnings and inaccurate information comes along for the ride. We may not even be fully aware of the inaccurate conclusions we made because our rational brain was not yet formed to help us evaluate or discern information. It wasn't online during those formative years.

OUR NEGATIVITY BIAS: SELECTIVE LEARNING

In their 2019 book, *The Power of Bad,* John Tierney and Roy Baumeister explain how our brains are more wired to pick up on and focus on the negative over the good. There's an evolutionary basis for this. Our ancestors were better able to survive and pass on their genes if they were alert and ready for threats and dangers. Over time, this wiring has been passed along generationally. The threats of today may not look like the ones of thousands of years ago, yet they feel and affect us with just the same intensity.

This negativity bias can be exacerbated by those experiences we encoded when we were young—those non-useful lessons. This can happen during times when, perhaps for our own good, our parents told us, "No!" or, "Don't touch that," or, "Don't do that." If there isn't enough balance between these negative messages and more encouraging ones, telling us how good we are, how well we are doing, and saying yes when appropriate, then we may develop a belief that we just aren't good enough.

I remember when I was learning how to swim. My dad would be in the pool with me and stand about four or five feet away with arms extended. "Okay, swim to me," he would say. And I would. As I got closer and closer and was about to reach him, he would back up. "Okay, now swim to me this far." So I would keep going. When I was about to reach him again, he would back up again. "Keep going, a little bit more." I'm so grateful that he did this in many ways. It showed me to always reach beyond what I think I am capable of; that, many times, we need to persevere through challenges and push further than we think possible. Yet, also, in those moments, I came away with some less than useful learnings. This was not because of my dad's approach; it was simply because, as we move through life, we will create our own stories that we alone are responsible for changing. The story I created was, "You haven't gone far enough. Just because you reached this point, doesn't mean you can stop; keep going, you need to keep going to be better."

These are small examples and, of course, not absolute. I was able to identify these as potential magnet mind programs—as I'll call them—because when I took the time to introspect and ask myself what inner voice was talking to me at certain times during my life and at certain key decision points, these examples came right up. That's how our subconscious magnet mind works. It always knows. It is always present, always there for us, and always wanting to protect us. While our conscious mind can only process 40 to 50 bits of information per second, our subconscious mind can process 11 million bits of information every second.

I saw this search for the negative occur in my adult life repeatedly. I would obsess over one or two critical comments on a performance review and magnify them to be larger than they were. I immediately jumped to the conclusion that one or two negative comments, even if in a sea of 10 or 20 positive ones, were evidence that I was not capable of doing my work anymore and that people wanted me to leave. I became lost in this abyss of self-doubt, and the feelings of inadequacy intensified. As philosopher Friedrich Nietzsche cautioned, "If you gaze into the abyss, the abyss gazes also into you." By understanding how this negativity bias works, we can decide to shift ourselves out of this abyss and away from these toxic thought patterns.

Before understanding the power of this negativity bias, no amount of conscious-mind coaching helped. Oh Suzy, I'd say to myself, you're just hard on yourself; focus on the good feedback. Or, you're such a type A perfectionist, of course you feel that way. Don't worry about it. Don't worry about it? Let me just say that, in any coaching, mentoring, or counseling session, the last thing anyone wants to hear is the phrase, "Oh, well, just don't worry about it."

The following is an activity that I use when this happens, and oh, it does happen. Even now, I find myself drifting toward the negative thought patterns, criticizing myself, or imagining the worst-case scenario. Here's what I do to get control of this negativity bias.

ACTIVITY: SHRINK THE NEGATIVE

Take a situation and ask yourself this question: Regarding this situation or event, what have I done that has been useful, helpful, and recognized as positive by others?

Write down as many examples as you can, and remember the positive words or reactions you received. For example, if the event is an annual evaluation, go through and highlight all of the positive comments or affirming feedback.

Then, on another piece of paper or section of a Word document, write out the negative comments that you heard or received. I know this may not be fun to write, but go ahead, and don't edit them. Write them out exactly, as the comments themselves are often less threatening than our reaction to them. After you have written down the actual comments and noticed how different they are from what your brain heard or told you, now assign a number to the intensity of those comments. In essence, how intensely negative do you feel about that comment now that you see it written out? For me, what starts as a nine or 10, or even 10+ when I first hear it, usually lowers to a four or a five when I see it written down or when I audit it against the comments I created in my own head.

Finally, take the number you wrote down and cut it in half. You could probably cut it in thirds given how much our mind magnifies the negative, but we'll settle for half. So, if it went from a 10 to a five, it's now a 2.5. Then reread all of the positive comments and information you have received about the situation. Assign a number to how you feel about those. Let's say the number is six. Great. Now double it to 12.

The point of this exercise is not to just add or subtract numbers. It's to reset and better calibrate the way we see ourselves and our world to counter our negativity bias. Of course, there will be times when we haven't handled an event very well, or when there are more negative than positive comments. The activity is still useful in that it helps us to see this in a nonthreatening way. If you find yourself in the middle of this type of situation, say, "Good, now I can create a new learning." Then write down all of the things you will do differently in the future, or that you can do *now* to fix the situation. Then assign a positive feeling to those improvement statements in the form of a number, and double it. See where this is going? We are intentionally taking control over our brain's negativity bias and choosing to rebalance it so more positive and useful learnings emerge as a guide.

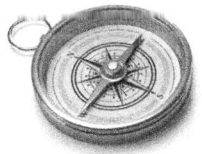

CHAPTER 5

RESHAPING OUR MEMORIES TO FREE OUR MINDS

What makes certain early experiences so powerful? The answer is memory. In this chapter, we'll explore how and why we form specific long-term memories and the way in which they shape how we see the world and ourselves. More importantly, we'll look at how memories can be reconsolidated—reframed and reshaped—to help us better control and interpret our responses.

MEMORY CONSOLIDATION AND EMOTION: STORING AND RECALLING

Think about what you had for dinner a week ago. Can you recall? Perhaps you can if it was a significant event, like a birthday or an anniversary. For most of us, if we didn't experience or associate a significant emotion with the event, it's unlikely to be retained in our long-term memory. Emotions are the very building blocks of memories, and they decide what is important enough to be stored and recalled.

Think of some intense or traumatic moments in your life.

Most of us can recall where we were when we heard about significant events in the news, like the *Challenger* exploding or the events of September 11th. When we experience an event with a high emotional charge—positive or negative—the brain's hippocampus makes sure we encode that memory. In this way, our memories are contextual.

Emotions are like a warning light on a car dashboard. It's as if they are saying to us, "Hey, wait, pay attention, something important is going on." If this was a negative event, and we experienced negative emotions (anger, sadness, rejection, fear), then that memory gets retained to form a warning system to protect us from this happening again. It's a survival lesson.

If we experienced positive emotions (joy, happiness, gratitude), our brain wants to remember this so we can recognize how and where to experience it again. When emotions are aroused, our memories are consolidated, meaning that these short-term, momentary experiences are transformed into more stable, long-term memories and stored. Our emotional response produces neurotransmitters or chemicals in our brain that facilitate this consolidation process. And, as you may have guessed, our brains tend to remember more negatively-charged events over positively-charged ones, because it's the negative ones that could pose more harm to our safety and well-being. This happens especially when our amygdala is aroused—the fear center in our brain, responsible for our fight-flight-or-freeze reactions.

Memories are stored in connections between our neurons. When a certain group of neurons are activated, a memory occurs. Our memories serve an adaptive role as we are growing up. They help us identify potential threats and dangers around us. Yet, our memories can be maladaptive as well. For example, if we experienced a traumatic event and are reliving it, the memories can prevent us from moving forward. This can lead to prolonged, long-term stress, as experienced by many victims of trauma, whether in childhood or adulthood.

ASSIGNING MEANING TO OUR MEMORIES

Memory occurs when our brains encode, store and then later retrieve experiences we have and information we take in. There are two types of memory: short-term and long-term. Short-term memory is our working memory. We use it in the moment to remember tasks, numbers, or take in information during a conversation. We may not need to store it longer than a few minutes or hours, hence why it's short-term. The second type of memory is long-term, which includes both our explicit memories of facts and events and our implicit, more autonomic memories, such as how we ride a bike or drive a car. Memories are consolidated from short-term to long-term based on if the brain determines the information is important for a future use or event.

But something else is happening in the process of memory consolidation—the assignment of meaning to that memory. We create an emotional learning. It's not just that we experience an intense emotion and our brain encodes the memory. At the same time, the brain then draws a conclusion because of that experience.

For example, when I was six, I regularly interacted with a group of neighborhood girls. They lived in the houses next door and across the street from mine. I considered one of the girls, Jamie, my very best friend. Jamie had the exact same birthday as mine, same day and same year. We always thought that was a fun coincidence. Our houses were right next door, and our bedroom windows lined up facing each other. Many days, after we finished playing outside, we would go home for dinner, then meet up at our windows after we ate. We spent many summer nights sitting in our own bedrooms and talking through our open windows.

One summer, I remember saving up my allowance and birthday money so I could buy one of those split-heart necklaces for Jamie and me. I wanted so much to have a best friend; someone who I could feel connected with every second as I wore that necklace. I don't remember exactly what happened to that necklace, or if Jamie ever wore her half.

One day, when we were playing outside with the larger group of neighborhood girls, one of the girls who lived across the street said to follow her because the group had a surprise for me. I wondered what it was. Maybe it's a present? Did they get me something? How special that they have something for me! I must be special!

We walked over toward Jamie's house. I was smiling inside. This has to be great, I thought. They told me to stand on the porch of one of their houses while they lined up on the walkway directly across from me. Jamie was lined up too, but for some reason she didn't seem to be smiling; she almost looked sad. I figured she was trying not to crack a smile to spoil the fun surprise. The other girl began counting to three, and after she said three, they all said in unison, "We hate you!"

Completely crushed, I stood there immobile for a few seconds. What just happened? Is this a joke? Do they really hate me? *Why* do they hate me? There's more of them than me. What if something is wrong with me? What if I am ..." My eyes swelled with tears. I felt this horrible sense of sadness and fear in my body. I was struggling to understand what had just happened. The girls had all walked off by now and were playing in another part of the yard. Did Jamie say it too? I don't remember if she did. She was standing next to them. But

I don't think she said anything. Still, she was standing there. And now she was gone; she went with them. My best friend just stood there while this happened to me and then she went off with them. I realized I was all alone.

The thoughts raced through my head so fast I probably didn't even realize I was thinking them. My brain assigned a meaning to this event based on my emotions and my accumulated experiences up to that point in time. I was six years old, so I didn't have the benefit of understanding human interaction and behavior. I didn't understand the concepts of teasing, or bullying, or self-confidence. All I knew was that this group of friends, including Jamie, whom I trusted and liked so much, just screamed that they hated me to my face. There was no reason, no fight, nothing that I recall even prompting it. It just came out of the blue. And it shocked my entire system.

While this event certainly wasn't among the worst that children, teenagers, or adults have faced, to my six-year-old, sensitive self, it was devastating. It was made worse by the fact that the person I had trusted the most, Jamie, who had the other half of my best-friend necklace, was part of this betrayal. My brain encoded this event in my memory and locked it in as one of the most impactful events in my life. It assigned meaning to attempt to make sense of why it happened; to create a lesson in the hope that the event wouldn't be repeated. The problem is, sometimes that lesson, the assigned meaning, is not accurate. Sometimes it's downright harmful, as it was in this case for me. I came away with the lesson that something was fundamentally wrong with me; that I must have done something or been someone to deserve this. It taught me that people I care about will betray and leave me, at any moment and without warning.

This deeply-rooted belief ended up influencing so many of my adult interactions, decisions, and relationships. My brain was constantly on guard, and I desperately wanted people to like me and not be upset with me. Even in high school, college, or as a young working adult, decades removed from this traumatic event that my six-year-old self experienced, that memory and the meaning assigned to it ran in the background of my mind. It impacted the way I perceived myself and my interpersonal relationships.

I noticed a few patterns in my life that I hypothesized stemmed from this event. One pattern was a constant fear that if I had a disagreement or conflict with someone, they would immediately hate me. This played out in my relationships and at my work. What could have been healthy dialogue, discussion, and communication, devolved quickly into tears, tension, and emotions. The second pattern was a belief that as soon as there was one disagreement in a relationship, it would end.

So, I began to expect that people close to me would eventually hate me or abandon me, just as Jamie had done that day. Therefore, when there was a difficult conversation or a need to communicate about an important matter, my protective shield would go up, and I would behave in ways that would cause the relationship or the interaction to go south. While this felt completely out of my control, I was actually the one propelling this cycle the whole time. This pattern impacted my work, my health, and my relationships. Our memories are among some of the most powerful drivers in our lives. If we are not aware of how they work, then they can control many of our decisions.

After one particular instance, one of my colleagues talked with me directly about a pattern he had observed with me in work situations. Knowing the story of Jamie and the neighborhood girls, he asked me if I had accepted and fully reconciled that event. Clearly, I had not, I said. The pattern he observed was an accurate one. In situations of intense interpersonal conflict at work, I would conclude that I wasn't good enough, that something was wrong with me, and that I needed to leave the situation (or organization), just like I felt on the porch that fateful summer day. This was an example of my brain repeating a pattern to keep me safe, and not necessarily to help me thrive, grow, and become my best self.

When thinking about these negative patterns, it's useful to look at the connection between thoughts, emotions, and memories. There's a huge difference between thinking and remembering, and we often confuse the two. Many times, we may believe we are thinking rationally and objectively, yet we are actually deep in remembering and pattern matching against old memories and experiences.

Thinking occurs on a more deliberate and self-reflective level. Remembering occurs as more of an emotional, immediate, and autonomic act. When we find ourselves stuck in patterns of remembering, our brain has created a well-worn, habitual path. It filters information and communication to be congruent with the emotions we feel and the belief system we have in place about ourselves, others, and the world, clashing with our independent thought process. It's why we tend toward confirmation bias and why the emotions we feel about someone directly influence how we perceive them and react in response. This is likely why it's often said that people remember how we make them feel more than what we say.

This process of pattern matching doesn't just happen in relation to negative memories. For intensely positive emotions, we may also draw conclusions or meanings which, again, aren't always accurate. For example, when I was growing up, my dad made sure to always ask his parents to call him when they arrived home after visiting us. Although the drive from our home to theirs wasn't that long, he would often secretly follow them home after they left, to make sure they got in safely.

As a young child, I remembered this because they told me they did it because they loved my grandparents so much. They said that's what you do when you love someone—you protect them and keep them safe. While there is certainly positive intent and a kernel of truth in this, one can see how my child mind interpreted this. Ah, this is what it means to care about someone. If someone loves you, they will follow you home and ask you to call them when you get there (not just in bad weather or late at night, but all the time). This is what it means to be loved. Those actions were encoded as loving, protective, and familiar, and I grew up looking for those behaviors in friends, family, and even in those I was dating as validation that they cared.

The important thing to keep in mind here is that this behavior was not all bad. The trouble is always in the extreme—in my young mind's conclusion that this action was required, all the time, to communicate love. I found myself being attracted to and dating people who displayed overly protective and, at times, possessive behavior. Conversely, I found myself losing interest in or distancing myself from good people who did not ask me to call them every time I drove home or who didn't think to follow me to make sure I arrived at my destination. I saw neglect in what was actually respect and freedom, and love in controlling behavior.

What does this tell us? When we are young, the meanings we assign to our memories are frequently incomplete and often incorrect. We can find ourselves surrounded by the same type of people, or reliving the same situation, feeling completely unable to stop these patterns from repeating. Yet, this is fully *within* our control. Our memories have been influencing how we assess the world and others, the way we see ourselves, and our decisions and conclusions.

PEARLS OF WISDOM: WHY OUR BRAINS DISTORT MEANING

We know that when we assign meaning to our memories or create an emotional learning, a lot can go wrong. But the interesting thing is that, quite often, there is a positive and useful learning hidden underneath. This positive learning is there to keep us safe so we can learn from our past and improve as we move into the future. It's there to protect us.

Take the previous scenario as an example. It might be that the pearl of wisdom is that it's useful for someone you love to confirm you've returned home safely if you leave late at night or in adverse weather conditions. So, why does this potentially useful process often get undermined and distorted by our subconscious mind?

Interestingly, it's because of the way the memory is formed. When we experience a situation or event that is painful, threatening, or scary, our subconscious mind wants us to remember the learning or pearl of wisdom that will ensure we don't experience the situation again. And so, it grabs everything that was going on around us at the time of the experience and wraps that around the learning, whether it is related to it or not, to fill up our early warning system.

Recall that any experience we have is processed through our five senses (sight, sound, touch, smell, and taste). This is why we sometimes have strong reactions or associations to smells, music and sound, or tastes. Yet the mind may grab too much, or it may form associations and meanings that are not fully accurate.

The process is much like how a pearl forms inside an oyster. When a foreign substance enters the oyster between the mantle and the shell, the mantle then secretes aragonite and conchiolin, the substances that are also present in the oyster's shell, to encase the irritant and protect the oyster. The pearl is actually the coating that the oyster produces to protect itself from the foreign irritant. The meanings we give to the events and adversities in our lives are like the coating the oyster uses to make the pearl. And those meanings can be useful or not, depending on how we choose to create them.

Now, you may be thinking, how can our subconscious mind grab too much? The answer lies in just how much information we take in consciously, compared to what we take in subconsciously and beyond our awareness. But how can these subconscious pieces of information bypass our five senses?

A 2013 study published in the *Journal of Neuroscience* found that even though a person's primary visual cortex was completely destroyed, in essence, they were blind, they were still processing visual information, even though they were not consciously aware or able to "see" it. The experimenters placed images of human faces in front of them whose eyes were either directly focused on or averted from the patient. Despite the fact the patient could not see these pictures the way we would think about sight and vision, MRI scans of their brain revealed a stronger amygdala reaction when shown pictures of faces with eyes looking at them directly (direct gaze). When they asked the patient to verbally respond to whether or not they thought the faces were looking directly at them, the answers were mixed; yet when they measured the activity in the brain directly, they found that there was a sense of perception occurring beyond conscious awareness that was consistent with the pictures that were being shown.

The researchers proposed that there may be a rapid subcortical pathway that communicates with our brain (specifically with the amygdala) when we perceive a threat. This pathway may bypass our primary visual cortex. In essence, it is why we may sense a possible threat before it actually occurs. It may also point to how neuroplastic our brains can be to rewire our neural network if one of our primary senses, in this case vision, is offline. Ironically, there may be a lot more to perception, than what we currently perceive.

THE MALLEABILITY OF MEMORY

When I began my research into locus of control, I never expected it would take me down the path of studying memory and how our memories of past events so significantly impact and shape our present and future reality. I saw memories as a recollection of what happened to us in the past that didn't change over time. After all, in all my graduate studies, memory was the one thing I relied on to help me learn, organize, and synthesize material. It almost seemed as if memories were analogous to files in a filing cabinet or on a computer. I thought of them as objective, immutable, and accessible when we wanted or needed them. Little did I know that was only a small part of the overall picture.

I came across research and studies on memory reconsolidation—the idea that memories are malleable and can be altered over time—which was a marked departure from prior scientific theory around memory encoding. In the 1990s, scientists concluded that emotional learnings were permanent and could not be changed in a person's lifetime. I was curiously excited about this and mildly unsettled at the same time. Everything that I had believed about memory was now in question. Yet there was something very freeing about this too. If the negative memories influencing some of my thoughts and decisions may not be entirely as I believed them to be, then the meanings I drew from these memories could be revised.

In *Memory Reconsolidation,* Cristina Alberini and Joseph LeDoux explain that new data has challenged the way we've always understood memory to work. Each time we access a memory, it is susceptible to being altered, and we're not consciously aware of this. Then, in its changed state, it is reconsolidated into long-term memory and available for future retrievals, where the process happens again. Like a stored file, it is opened, edited, and then resaved. Memories are therefore not fixed and immutable snapshots of our past. They are dynamic and susceptible to new information, emotions, and encodings each time we access them.

What this also tell us is that memories are not objective and may be inaccurate. Massive amounts of important and contextual information from these memories may have been deleted, distorted, or generalized over time. Then, each time we access these memories, our brains reassess and re-encode, altering them again.

It's important to understand just how prone to inaccuracy our most powerful memories can be. The emotions we are experiencing at the time have the ability to influence how these memories are first encoded and consolidated, and then reconsolidated. This is critical as it's likely that most of us will be recalling painful experiences when we are in a depressed or painful state, thus compounding the negative emotions and negative reconsolidation.

It occurred to me that I had likely been doing passive memory reconsolidation for most of my life. Unaware of the science or the details of how this process actually worked, I'd access a prior memory while in an emotional state (likely negative or non-useful) similar to the one I was in at the time the memory was first created. For example, when I recalled the memory of

Jamie joining the neighborhood kids in screaming that they hated me, it was generally when I was feeling sad, scared, or abandoned by a friend or loved one. That childhood event then became amplified and distorted by more negative emotions and the meaning was strengthened in my subconscious: I'm unlovable. People only pretend to care about me. They will hate me. They will eventually leave me. I will be all alone.

Conversely, if you are remembering an old trauma in a safe space and with the mindset that it helped you positively grow because of the lessons you learned from it, you may be able to reframe the past experience as being useful to developing you into the person you are today.

This process is explored in Paul Ekman's 2007 book, *Emotions Revealed*, where he explains that talking about a past emotional experience can actually trigger that emotion in the present moment. He points out how powerful and automatic this emotional remembering can be and how a negative emotion can impact how we continue to remember an event, furthering that feedback loop.

Ekman explains that we don't bother to consciously challenge if the feeling is valid or not, yet our subconscious mind seeks out and filters only confirming information. We then end up evaluating the situation only in a way that is congruent with the emotion. Ekman also proposes a sort of refractory state when we are in the grip of this emotional remembering. In this state, we are less likely to incorporate new information that does not fit our negative narrative, and so we need to step away from it in order to reframe our experiences.

This concept of the malleability of memory opens up a whole new world of possibility. Each time we access a memory, we have the potential to call it up from its storage space, reconsolidate it with the new information available to us at the time (usually when we are older and wiser), and then update the meaning or conclusion formed as a result of the memory.

Memory reconsolidation means we no longer need to be controlled by our memories, the emotions that have intensified them, or the meanings we have assigned to them. We are free to understand our memories are imperfect and often distorted or inaccurate recollections of events that occurred in our past. And, even if these events were negative and emotionally charged, we are able to assign new meanings to the memories when we are in a more positive state, so that we can improve our lives. We have the freedom to reconsolidate these as learnings in ways that affirm how we have grown and changed our lives for the better because of our past experiences.

MEMORY RECONSOLIDATION: PUTTING IT INTO PRACTICE

How do we do this in practice?

Daniela Schiller, who, at the time of writing, leads the Schiller Laboratory of Affective Neuroscience at the Ichan School of Medicine at Mount Sinai, focuses her research on emotional learning and memory. She's given several brilliant lectures, available online, where she explains how humans can overcome the fear response through reconsolidated learning.

In an article in *Nature*, entitled "Preventing the Return of Fear in Humans Using Reconsolidation Update Mechanisms," Schiller and her colleagues explain how we can update our memories from the older, fear-based ones to newer, more useful ones during this reconsolidation window. Their research shows how, by doing this, it is possible to eliminate the fear response people may have when they recall such memories.

This finding is even more important when we consider how our brains organize and stack similar experiences and memories over time. If we can change a powerful, fear-based memory into a more useful learning, then all the negative learnings connected to it change as well. There is a cumulative, positive effect.

Let's look at another method. In 2012, researchers Bruce Ecker, Robin Ticic, and Laurel Hulley wrote the book *Unlocking the Emotional Brain: Eliminating Symptoms at Their Roots Using Memory Reconsolidation*. They outlined memory reconsolidation as an effective means of producing transformational change in psychotherapy. Knowing that memories are capable of being re-encoded after they are accessed in the brain, the authors suggest that this method can both destabilize and then recode an emotional learning.

First, the person needs to access the emotional learning that is causing them harm. Next, they need to experience something new that will teach them a positive lesson in contrast to their harmful emotional learning. This experience needs to be vivid and in sharp juxtaposition to the first memory. Finally, this new experience needs to be repeated several times during the reconsolidation window.

We can walk through this with a hypothetical example. Let's say you had a negative experience presenting a work idea to a group of colleagues. You may have been nervous, stumbled over your words, forgot some of your main points, or perhaps their reactions to your presentation fell short of your expectations. Your brain then creates the conclusion (i.e., an emotional learning) that you aren't good at your job or valued by your colleagues. You may not even be fully aware that this emotional learning was created, yet it was. Then, later on at work, the memory shows up in different ways. For example, you may lack confidence in future presentations or avoid them altogether. More subtly, you may feel that your work is never good enough or that you could not possibly be competent in your role.

Ecker's framework would have you access the original learning where that memory was first encoded. It would then ask you to vividly remember other examples of when you did master a project or task at work, or when someone told you how intelligent and valuable you were. You would bring up that entire experience in vivid detail and reexperience how you felt emotionally. Critically, you would draw new conclusions consistent with that juxtaposed learning: You are good at your work; you are intelligent; your colleagues are very impressed with you and your ability.

Ecker and his colleagues explain how memory reconsolidation accesses and unlocks the neural synapses of the emotional learning. These learnings are stored in our implicit memory and form the building blocks of mental models that we create about ourselves and the world.

One important point Ecker noted is that memory reconsolidation will not interfere with autobiographical learning. If there were competencies or information we learned apart from the implicit emotional learning, those would be retained. Memory reconsolidation only impacts the implicit emotional learning, or the conclusions and schemas our brains formed from the intense, emotional event. When we target this old learning and then repeatedly focus on the new learning, memories are reconsolidated in this more positive emotional state. The old, non-useful schema can then be deleted.

Of course, it's best to be guided by a trained clinician through the process of memory reconsolidation. Yet, simply by becoming aware of how this process works and knowing the frameworks available, we become empowered to reexamine the non-useful learnings stored in our implicit memory that may be holding us back. We can visualize and imagine the gaps in our experiences and rewrite the meanings of our past. Imagination is a powerful force to help us envision and reinvent our future.

Let's consider how our imagination can help guide us in creating a new emotional learning; one that is more useful to the person we wish to become today. In therapy, I spent considerable time accessing that infamous memory of being six years old and having my friends chant, "We hate you." Working with my therapist, we went through every excruciating detail of that day and event as I recalled it as an adult, meaning I recognized that the memory and the images of that day had been altered and changed throughout my life. I imagined the me of today, older, wiser, and stronger, appearing in that scene right before it happened. The me of today took the hand of my six-year-old self, told her how incredible and wonderful she was, and that I would always be here to love her, help her, and support her. I told her I cared for her so much that I came back in time to tell her all of this and more.

Hand in hand, she and I walked through the neighborhood. As we did, my six-year-old friends smiled and waved at us, saying hello and telling my younger self how lucky I was to have someone who cared so much for her. She and I walked and talked. I told her everything she would need to know; the wonderful things that she would do, the challenges she would encounter, and the lessons she would learn from them. I told her that I would be with her every day, that she would never be alone, and that she and I, together, would have an amazing life.

In my imagination, we spent hours walking, talking, and squeezing each other's hands, so grateful and so full of love and care for one another. Then, as we were walking, one of the neighborhood kids came up to us and said, "Hey, we have a surprise for you both. Can you follow me?" And we did. We stood on the porch, and the kids lined up opposite us. Jamie was there, too, but this time she was smiling. And then, on the count of three, they all yelled, "We like you!"

Now, I understand this may sound a bit sappy, but this exercise empowered me to rewrite the learning I had created from that event. Not only did it associate a positive, warm emotion with that day (the memory image of my older, wiser, and stronger self giving reassurance to my younger self), but it reframed the challenges I would face in my life as opportunities, and it told my younger self something that it may not have known: that I survived that moment in time and would go on to thrive in my life because of it.

REWRITING OUR EMOTIONAL LEARNINGS

Can we really rewrite original learnings? In *Thinking, Fast and Slow*, Kahneman mentions an experiment to measure what happens when people change their minds over a certain belief that they once held. Once they successfully changed their belief, they were then asked to report the belief that they previously held before they made the change. It demonstrated that if we completely adopt a new belief or world view, so much so that this is deeply ingrained in our subconscious mind, in essence, an internal paradigm shift, we will forget ever even holding the prior viewpoint. It would seem as foreign to us as if we never held it at all. The key is in the word *belief*. Beliefs are deeper than thoughts; they are driven by our perceptions, and they feel like an extension of us.

When we change a belief, something occurs in our brain that is almost like a neurological resonance. A neural pathway that is rewired and reconnected. For example, for the first few years of my marriage, I believed my husband and I would never be a "fit." I believed we were not fundamentally "compatible" and that we would always struggle or feel "mismatched." I placed some words here in quotes because I noticed how interesting they were; they opened a window into my old thought patterns. I had a belief system around what it meant for a relationship to "fit" or be "compatible." Fit what? And what was compatibility? Was it static or does it develop and deepen over time?

Some 15 years later, I have completely different beliefs. My wiring on this has changed, and the negative emotions stemming from the old beliefs have been eradicated at the root. While I can recall some of the words and phrases I used to use, it's nearly impossible for me to think the same way I thought during those first few years.

Importantly, if we forget even holding this prior viewpoint, then the negative meanings and memories we encoded around the old viewpoint also shift. We stop seeing them as factual events that happened to us in our lives. Rather, we accept that our *brain* decided what happened to us and what meaning it would have for us—then and now. The memory was encoded at the point of the event, and the meaning and belief system around that event were formed. When we update the belief system and the meaning we attached to it, we change the very essence of the memory.

HOW OUR BODIES HOLD MEMORIES

What happens in our mind and body after a traumatic event is truly extraordinary. At the very root of our most traumatic experiences are direct and serious threats to our safety or security. However, it's important to note that a trauma may not have been an event that *actually* threatened our security or safety; it need only be that our mind and body perceived and believed it did.

Brent Baum is a trauma and addiction therapist who has served as clinical director for several trauma centers throughout the United States. He developed a highly effective process called Holographic Memory Resolution® (HMR), designed to reframe and resolve traumatic memories so they cannot hurt us anymore. You can read more about Brent Baum and HMR by going to www.healingdimensions.com.

I had the privilege of working with Brent during my research, and I experienced a session of HMR firsthand. I highly recommend his work, especially if you have experienced traumatic events. Baum has given several lectures on the nature of trauma and what happens in the mind and body. In fact, he calls it the mind-body because they are inextricably connected in the way they experience and then process traumatic events.

He explains that as we experience a trauma, our system is monitoring the events and the timeline leading up to the events and then right after. If the moment of the most intense trauma is T_{10}, it's likely that we won't remember the most intense point: our conscious system shuts off. Our brains have the ability to pause consciousness when we are feeling overwhelmed and do not have the tools or resources to cope with the situation at hand. However, if we survive, we may remember certain elements of T_8 or T_9 because, after the event, our brain made sure to record what happened leading up to the intense trauma. It takes a mental snapshot. All of this happens quickly, subconsciously, and automatically.

This framework captures our brain wave patterns and any and all physiological tension or pain that we feel at the time. This is a protection mechanism and creates a state-bound or state-dependent memory, meaning we may be able to remember, and feel within our body, more information about those moments if we are in a similar mental or physical state as when we originally encoded the memory. This whole-body experience is stored in neural pathways throughout our body, not just in the memory center of our brains. This may explain phantom limb pain. Even though someone's limb has been amputated, there are still messages being sent from the nerves near the limb to the brain as if the limb was still there.

Imagine, then, if this recording is like a repeat loop, stored in our mind and body, like a program running in the background. Why? So it can form a learning, an implicit memory, to keep us safe for the future. In order to do this and make sure we never get close to T8 or T9 again, it stores this trauma somatically. Baum explained that he has worked with individuals who had chronic leg or back pain with no medically diagnosable cause. Through HMR, they were able to resolve the pain because they worked through the traumatic memories that had become trapped in a location in the body related to or connected with the trauma, even if that location was not permanently injured from the trauma.

The premise for this work is that our bodies are representations and embodiments of what is in our energy field. And our thoughts, beliefs, and perceptions shape and influence that energy field. When we have negative beliefs and thoughts, whether we are consciously aware of these or not, they affect everything within our energy field and then are reflected in our physical state.

How do these negative thoughts and beliefs get so deeply encoded within our subconscious and then within our energy field? Trauma. Baum proposed a theory of trauma encoding that would explain how the way we think about what happened to us can impact the way we move through the world and, ultimately, the results we see in our lives. His theory explains that, as we are experiencing a trauma, our neurology monitors what is taking place. It is aware of the emotional spike that corresponds to the traumatic event.

Many times, there are good lessons associated with this safety program. For example, if we experienced a car accident because we were distracted while driving, the program can help us recognize and guard against those distractions in the future. At the same time, this safety program can also hold us back from reaching our full potential.

Imagine if we had a traumatic experience with public speaking or presenting to an audience. Our brains may remember all of the factors leading up to the traumatic experience, even down to the feeling in our bodies and what our senses were perceiving (time of year, sounds, sights, smells). When we are in the situation again, even if it is now harmless, we may instinctively feel under threat and either avoid it altogether or be unable to perform. Because of this, the body can be a useful indicator of when we are experiencing stress or anxiety that feels out of our control. It's an automatic feeling, one we don't want to have, yet we cannot seem to remove it—the result of a holographic memory stored within us.

To change the feeling, we have to first understand what trauma program is running, what it's trying to keep us safe from, and how we can assure ourselves that we are in fact okay and that we don't need to have this program running in order to survive. One way to do this is to state aloud the important lesson that we don't want to forget so we can retain that and let the traumatic part of the learning go. In this way, we can choose upon a new and useful meaning as we let the rest of the program go.

CHAPTER 6

THE CONNECTION BETWEEN MIND AND BODY

Throughout this book, we've discussed how connected the functions of our mind and body can be. In Chapter 4, we saw how the physiology of our brain affects how we learn and create beliefs. And, in Chapter 5, we learned how our bodies can store emotions and memories. Now, let's take a look at how this mind- body interconnection works. Can our anxieties actually affect our well-being? How do our emotions present themselves physically? If our subconscious beliefs do impact our health, then can we take back control and give ourselves a better life? Let's start with an example that sheds some light on the power of the magnet mind.

IS MY ANXIETY MAKING ME SICK?
In July 2020, during the global COVID-19 pandemic, I had an intense and rapid onset of vertigo. While I had experienced a few mild waves of dizziness in my life before, none of them were as severe as this. After 30 minutes of writhing on the floor, dry heaving from nonstop nausea, and feeling a sense

of complete disorientation, I called EMS and they took me to the ER by ambulance.

The hospital ran a full battery of tests, found nothing definitive, and sent me home with headache medication, concluding it was likely a combination of headache-induced vertigo and mild dehydration. While the intense vertigo did pass, there was lingering episodic dizziness that occurred for about two months after this event, especially when trying to use the computer and join virtual, on-screen meetings.

Around this time, I was also going through a comprehensive interview process for a new position. It didn't occur to me that this may have played a role in my symptoms. Yet the coincidence wasn't lost on me that while I was weighing up whether to make a significant career change—a stress-inducing process for most people—I experienced an intense disruption to my balance and physical stability. I wondered if there could be a subconscious emotional corollary to how I was feeling physically. Could there be a connection between this physical event and what I was feeling on a deep, emotional level? Was my stress and anxiety making me sick?

Then, another memory. I was in sixth grade and having trouble with friends. The girls I was hanging out with had begun to form a tight clique, and I was on the outside. I noticed myself feeling the familiar terror I'd felt in the situation with Jamie and the neighborhood kids. It was happening again.

Suddenly I began "getting sick" and needing to stay home. I complained about a myriad of stomach problems, likely caused by the fear and anxiety. My mom took me to every doctor she could, and I had more exams, X-rays, and ultrasounds than I can recall. My parents were terrified that I had some horrible disease. While I didn't relish the taste of the strawberry barium that I needed to drink prior to X-rays, or having to hold a full bladder before the ultrasounds, I was very happy that I could stay home and away from school during this time. I didn't have to face the issues with my friends or worry about them bullying or abandoning me.

Years later, I read a book called *The Great Pain Deception*. The author, Steve Ozanich, explains how sometimes our bodies manifest painful or irritating symptoms to protect us from our deepest fears and anxieties. The symptoms create the need for us to be careful, play it safe, or adjust our lifestyle, and thus we are able to retreat into our comfort zone and allay our fears. The reality was that, all those years ago, my brain was subconsciously saying, "Ah, we found a solution. We are keeping you safe. You can stay home. Away from people who can hurt you."

These two memories were extremely enlightening. Our thoughts and emotional states can express themselves as physical symptoms designed to protect and keep us safe.

Let's explore this idea further. When we feel a strong emotion, we can usually identify a place in our body where that emotion lives. In this way, emotions have a physical resonance to them. For me, anxiety and worry resided in the pit of my stomach. Fear was in my head and my chest. And I can feel gratitude and love in my heart area. It's amazing how these emotions take up residence in our physical bodies.

In his book, *The Body Keeps the Score*, Bessel van der Kolk explains how our brain responds to traumatic occurrences by producing a heightened stress response to people or events we encounter through our lives. This response is stored and experienced in our bodies. Over time, if we don't heal our earlier traumas, they will exact a physical toll on us.

I've seen examples of this in my own life as well. Ever since I can remember, I've struggled with stomach and digestion issues. They surface when I am anxious, afraid, or worried.

If you are in a fight with a friend or coworker and start to feel emotions building, like anger or fear, ask yourself where you feel that emotion in your body. Most of us will be able to identify a somatic location.

The pathway between our emotions and this somatic response can run in either direction. Amy Cuddy, in her 2012 TED Talk, "Your Body Language May Shape Who You Are," described research that she and her colleagues conducted on what happens alchemically in our body when we alter our physical stature. She explained that when a person holds a power pose, with both hands extended up in the air while standing up straight, their body will naturally produce powerfully invigorating chemicals that can instill courage and confidence. This suggests there is a feedback loop between our physical body and our emotional state. Conversely, there is also an internal reaction in our bodies to negative physical states. For example, if we assume a slouched or defeated posture, slumping our shoulders and lowering our heads, our bodies will respond by producing negative emotions as well.

What does this all suggest? We may, in fact, have more control over our health and well-being than we previously had thought.

EPIGENETICS: WHAT DETERMINES OUR HEALTH?

Bruce Lipton is a cellular biologist by training and was teaching at the University of Wisconsin's School of Medicine at a time when the accepted medical science said that genes determined nearly every aspect of our lives. Illness and disease were seen to be the result of genetic programming turning itself on or off at any given time.

If we accept genetic determinism and the primacy of DNA, we must accept that human beings have little control over their health and well-being. It was believed that our genes controlled our destiny and that we were victims of what we inherited from our parents. While it's obvious that genetics can play a role, Dr. Lipton's work shows us that the impact it has is much less than we may have originally thought. In his bestselling book, *The Biology of Belief,* he explains that our genes and DNA do not necessarily determine our health outcomes.

In 1967, Dr. Lipton worked on an experiment that demonstrated evidence for what science would later validate as epigenetics. He had grown three distinct dishes of stem cells, and each dish had identical cells to the originating parent cell. One dish had muscle cells, one bone, and one fat. Cells live in what is called a culture medium which contains nutrients such as amino acids that are necessary for microbial growth and division.

Dr. Lipton found that when he extracted just the culture mediums from each dish and combined them with synthetic blood (to simulate the body's natural internal environment), the culture medium in which a stem cell was placed determined what the cell would become. For example, initially he took the culture medium from the dish that had previously grown thousands of muscle cells. He then combined that medium with synthetic blood. He found that, whatever type of stem cell he placed *into* that medium (bone or fat, for example), the cells divided and still became muscle cells, mirroring the previous environment. It was the medium, the environment surrounding the cell, that influenced what it became.

This groundbreaking research challenged the science of genetic determinism that was being taught in medical schools and even, ironically, in the same medical school where Dr. Lipton had been teaching. Our genes play a role, yet they are not the sole determinant of our physical reality. Instead, it may be, as Nijhout suggested in "Metaphors and the Role of Genes in Development," that our genes are not ultimately in control of changes or expressions of our cells. Rather, within certain environments or contexts, they can be prompted to catalyze such change.

This is important because we can work to control the environment and the context in which the genes operate. This idea that something "above" or "on top of" (epi) our genes may control the way they are expressed and the health outcomes we see has tremendous implications. This experiment might feel a bit disconnected from our day-to-day lives, but, in reality, it means we have a significant amount of control over our health. The key is gaining more influence over both our internal and external environments.

Our internal cultural medium is the environment within our body—our blood and the chemicals and hormones within it. Our cells have receptors that receive signals from that environment and then those signals impact the cell's cultural medium and the expression of its genes and DNA. When we are stressed or anxious, the levels of stress hormones such as cortisol, adrenaline, and norepinephrine can create an unhealthy environment for our cells. The cultural medium of our blood signals to our cells that they need to go into protection mode. Cells can't be in protection mode at the same time as growth or regeneration mode. When they're not able to replicate and regenerate, they are prone to mutation and cellular damage. They can't perform the normal functions that cells must undertake to be healthy. This can then precipitate physical symptoms, illness, and disease.

We've probably all heard that stress negatively impacts our immune systems. In fact, when doctors are doing organ transplants, they often give patients stress hormones to shut off their immune systems so the organ won't be rejected right away. This is why we tend to catch colds or the flu more easily when we are under stress, not getting enough sleep (which is restorative for our mind and body), and not feeding our body with healthy foods to support our internal environment.

The second environment is our external one. For example, the air around us, the water we drink and come into contact with, what we place on our skin, or what we take in through eating and drinking. This is why the environment around us is so important. All of this plays a role in our overall health and well-being.

CONTROLLING OUR INTERNAL AND EXTERNAL ENVIRONMENTS

What this research tells us is that we are not just a brain attached to a physical body. Our entire system and neurology are interconnected. Everything operates, or doesn't, together. To improve our health, we must treat both the mind *and* body.

In contrast, as Lipton pointed out, modern medicine takes a more reductionist, Newtonian approach to analyzing and treating the body. There is an attempt to explain biological processes by laws of physics that can be observed and explained. If we can "take it apart" into its component pieces, we can study how it works. Yet, as Aristotle alluded to, we are all more than the sum of our parts.

In Newtonian mechanics, there's a focus only on the physical matter we can see before us: on an X-ray, for example, or a CT scan or MRI. It may not always factor in what we don't see—the internal, emotional environment, or the beliefs and perceptions that create an energetic resonance in the field around us. We think that because we cannot see this, it isn't real. And, yet, we see it in the patterns and results we get in our lives. We attract what is in harmony with our beliefs about ourselves and the world, and this, in turn, impacts our health and well-being. We become what we believe we are and what we believe we *will* be.

Dr. Lipton explained that our cells are, in essence, scanning their environment to determine how they will change to match and align with it. This sounds similar to the way our conscious mind filters information and forms conclusions based on how our perceptual filters encode the information. Lipton takes this a step further. He explains how, at a cellular level, our bodies operate similar to a computer. He likens the cell membrane to the central processer. Data enters through the cell's surface. The cell then behaves in a congruent way with the signals it receives from the environment.

We are not just reading our environment; we are downloading into our system. If we are surrounded by negative or angry people, situations, or events, then this type of information produces and releases stress hormones such as cortisol into our bloodstream which are then sent into our cells through the cellular membrane. The cell then responds accordingly.

Our physical health is a reflection of what data we are putting into the machine. We can become, down to a cellular level, a reflection of the environment we are in. This is why when we are in intense, volatile, and high-stress situations for prolonged periods of time, our physical system responds accordingly.

Cortisol and other stress hormones negatively impact digestion and heart rate, and they can increase headaches or body pains. The body feels like it must be in protection mode, conserving its energy for a perceived threat, and thus doesn't carry out important restorative functions like sleep, digestion, and proper circulation.

When our bodies are expending energy without adequate rest and recovery, our health and immunity decline. For example, there's a high prevalence of anxiety and depression among individuals who suffer from IBS, suggesting that this may be stress-induced—a physical manifestation of the internal environment. Additional studies further suggest a correlation between early infantile and childhood trauma and IBS symptoms in adulthood.

If our external environment and our beliefs have such a big impact on our health by way of our cells' receptors, what are we waiting for? Surely, we now have the power to take control and improve our well-being?

Some of you may be thinking: This is all well and good, but I don't think I can take control of my environment. This takes us right back to locus of control—whether we *believe* we have control or not.

The truth is, we do have control over our internal and external environments. We may not always feel like we do, yet we do have the ability to change the beliefs and perceptions that drive our emotions and impact how we react to a person or situation. We can use more positive emotions to shift how we are feeling, thinking, perceiving, and experiencing a life event, and we can disrupt the negative patterns. In this way, we produce less harmful stress chemicals and more positive, healthy ones such as serotonin, dopamine, and oxytocin. This, in turn, creates a healthier and more favorable environment in which our cells live, grow, and regenerate.

We also have the ability to change our external environment: our physical and mental habits, the people we interact with, and the jobs and work we do. This may not be easy, and it may mean making difficult decisions or thinking creatively in order to meet financial and other obligations. If it's important enough to our well-being, however, we will find a way.

We can change the internal, physical representation by ensuring the environment we are in, the people we are around, and the thoughts that form in our mind are healthy, positive, and productive. Often, the negativity we believe and perceive to be around us, may in fact be coming from our own destructive thought patterns about others or our situation. Even so, we control whether we choose to stay in a job or a relationship, or whether we choose to eat healthy foods and take care of our physical fitness.

In her book, *The Power Is Within You*, Louise Hay proposed that we all have control over contributing to every physical, mental, and emotional condition in our lives—for good or for bad. We do this with our thoughts, which then create our feelings, which generate emotions and shape our beliefs. In Hay's other book, Heal Your Body, she cataloged a list of health challenges and illnesses with their corresponding, underlying emotional cause. You can also find this list online by visiting www.alchemyofhealing.com.

So, it's clear we *can* gain greater control over our internal and external environment. However, it's also the *belief* that we have control (i.e., an internal locus) that has an impact on our physical and mental health. Several studies have shown that having an internal locus of control has a moderating effect on stress, anger, and depression. A study published in the *Procedia-Social and Behavioral Sciences* by Atefe Abdolmanafi, Mohamad Ali Besharat, Hojatollah Farahani, and Mohamad Reza Khodaii entitled "The moderating role of locus of control on the relationship between anger and depression in patients with major depressive disorder" showed a relationship between locus of control orientation and levels of anger and depression. Those with a higher internal locus of control tended to experience less depression and anger-causing situations than those with an external locus of control.

Another study from *Work & Stress*, An International Journal of Work, Health & Organisations by Jim Cvetanovski and Steve M. Jex looked at the relationship between locus of control and both psychological and physical well-being among 190 unemployed individuals. It found that having an internal locus of control was associated with higher levels of self-esteem and overall life satisfaction, as well as lower levels of depression and anxiety.

In addition, a 2011 article published on www.unhealthywork.org by Erin Wigger explains the association between locus of control and cardiovascular health, especially healthy behaviors that may also portend better outcomes for smoking cessation, weight loss, and other positive fitness behaviors. Wigger explains that individuals with an internal locus of control tend to engage in more healthy cardiovascular behaviors and therefore enjoy better heart health.

THE IMPACT OF OUR BELIEFS ON OUR PHYSICAL REALITY

I had heard the mantra, "Mind over matter," too many times to count. Despite learning of Dr. Lipton's theories and the interconnectedness of the mind and body, I was still skeptical. Could our beliefs really change the physical reality we experience? I felt it might give me false hope to believe this, and it seemed to discount a lot of traditional, diagnostic medical science. Just then, it was as if the universe placed an interesting experience in my path to prove a point.

It was mid-2019, and I had just reordered a new set of contacts. They were the same brand and same prescription as the ones I had before. I have daily contacts, so I'd wear them during the day and then dispose of them every evening. They came in two large boxes, with four smaller boxes of right and left lenses in each. I quickly removed one box from each of the larger boxes and arranged them systematically in the drawer of my bathroom vanity. I had a system set up so that I could easily pick out the relevant lens for each eye. The box for my right eye lens was on the right, and the box for my left eye lens was on the left. It is important to note here that the prescription difference between my lenses is significant, and my right eye has a slight astigmatism as well.

For two weeks, I wore the contacts. They worked perfectly and fit so comfortably. When I began to run out of the ones in the smaller boxes, I went into the linen closet to get more. It was then that I realized something astonishing. I had mixed up the right and left contacts in my bathroom drawer. The script power numbers were the exact opposite of what they should have been, and I noticed this when I saw the other boxes had an R and L on them to indicate the correct eye and lens. I went back to the drawer to confirm this, as it seemed completely unbelievable to me that I had been reversing my prescription in each eye and yet I had been able to see perfectly fine. Was this even possible?

I figured there must have been some odd mistake. Perhaps the ones in the drawer were correct and only that one sleeve was mismarked? I tried the lenses from the bathroom vanity on again. This time, I could barely see. I was incredulous. How in the world was it possible that I saw perfectly with these lenses in the wrong eyes for weeks?

To this day, I still cannot explain this. I know it occurred because, as I was realizing what happened, I slowed down to make absolutely sure I was understanding and checking every step. Sure enough, when my brain deeply believed I was putting in the correct lenses, my physical body actually changed to align with this belief.

As soon as that belief was shaken by seeing the boxes in the linen closet and realizing I had reversed them, my eyes no longer continued adjusting for the incorrect lenses. I did try to replicate this experiment again, even by mixing up the contacts randomly. Yet my brain knew that I was attempting to trick myself. When I later asked my doctor how this could happen, she said it was possible my brain and visual cortex were able to adjust. Unusual, yet possible.

The brain has also evolved to conserve energy. Therefore, it adapts and incorporates that which is predictable and expected. In this way, it saves energy because what is expected doesn't require the brain to expend energy or to fire neurons that trigger our attention. Our brain likes predictable and repeatable patterns, so much so that it will seek to create them from our prior experience to predict future outcomes. And, the brain adjusts only when it is surprised. Perhaps this explains my own experience with the contact lenses. Putting in my contacts has become a very automated act. I've been doing it for decades, and so my brain has deep wiring to expect that when I place them in my eyes, I will see clearly. That expectation was predicted by the brain and therefore expected. As such, it adapted and adjusted the visual cortex to meet that expectation. Now, there has been no clinical study done to test this hypothesis. It's simply an unexpected experiment that I had no intention of running that may shed light on how powerful and adaptable our brains really are.

This was a bit of a turning point for me. I experienced firsthand this connection between mind and body and the role that my beliefs and expectations had in shaping my physical reality. When unwell, my first thought had always been to focus on fixing the physical symptom. It's only been in the last few years that I began paying attention to the underlying emotional issue as well. Sometimes, it just wants our attention. So, we can ask it: What is the lesson you want to teach me? What is it you want me to know or do? Many times, it's the pearl of wisdom our body wants to remind us of before it can let the physical symptom go.

THE POWER OF ENTRAINMENT: ATTRACTING POSITIVE OR NEGATIVE ENERGY

Thanks to Dr. Lipton's work, we know that a cell's environment determines how it develops and what it eventually becomes. Kendall Powell's 2005 article in the well-respected scientific journal *Nature*, entitled "It's the Ecology, Stupid!" goes a little further, explaining how an organism's evolution is impacted not only by its physical environment but also by other living things around it. During the first few months that we are developing in the womb, our genes may control most of the wiring pattern of the brain. After that, our experiences and environment shape and reshape our existing neural circuits. This highlights the importance of the environment we choose to be in and the people with whom we choose to interact.

We know that our beliefs and emotions can create a positive or negative energy that drives our life outcomes, whether it's our physical health, our relationships, or our opportunities at work. But we are not islands. We affect and are affected by the people around us. Our inner environment helps to create our outer environment—the people we connect with.

You've probably heard of the phrase, "Birds of a feather flock together." Or, when you were growing up, perhaps one of your parents said, "Be careful of the company that you keep." There's truth to this. We tend to attract and surround ourselves with friends, peers, and colleagues who resonate and align with our own subconscious views of ourselves and of the world. That's why persistently negative people tend to hang out together, and why positive, high-performing people attract more positive high performers as well. We've seen this phenomenon play out around us. Groups of people, either at work, in school, or within communities, seem to communicate, think, or behave in similar ways. This is not simply a coincidence.

Did you know that there is a law of physics behind this? It's called entrainment, and it's the tendency of two oscillating or vibrating frequencies to harmonize together. You can see how this works by searching YouTube or the Internet for the term *metronomes entrainment*. The videos show metronomes in close proximity to one another oscillating to different frequencies. Within a few minutes, they all entrain together. Why does this happen?

Metronomes are matter. They are made of molecules and emit energy. Therefore, they are drawn to and affected by each other's frequencies. The same is true for us as human beings. We have a physical, energetic body. Our energy and emotions determine the frequency we produce. Just like the metronomes, we will entrain with the energy and frequencies we surround ourselves with. We will also attract that type of energy and frequency into our lives. As Albert Einstein said: "our separation from each other is an optical illusion. When something vibrates, the electrons of the entire universe resonate with it. Everything is connected. The greatest tragedy of human existence is the illusion of separateness."

Here is an example of entrainment that stood out for me. When you read it, think about times in your life—whether at work or with family—that you may have experienced this too. It occurred when a university I worked for merged with another university. As the merger was taking place, I met and connected with new colleagues. Two of them became my close friends: Dan and Bernard (who went by his nickname, Boom). Dan and Boom were innovative, future-focused, optimistic thinkers. They were on fire talking about fresh ideas, entrepreneurial inventions, and new ways of teaching and learning. Their energy was positive, collaborative and encouraging.

I liked who I was around them, and I noticed myself feeling

smarter and more empowered. They didn't talk negatively about people or situations. In fact, many times they shifted me during our conversations if I began to fall into a more critical mindset. They each had a high internal locus of control and took radical responsibility for their work and their results.

Boom was an educational innovator, author of several books, and a sought-after speaker on educational technology, innovation, and nontraditional models of teaching and learning. His research and scholarship focused on developing more learner-centric models for grading, and he challenged me to think about how I taught my students. When I decided to focus my dissertation on innovative and entrepreneurial operating models for twenty-first century higher education, Boom immediately agreed to serve on my committee. He freely gave his time to mentor me and help me shape my research question and methodology.

Dan worked in biotech in California and knew how to raise venture capital and pitch to investors. He was the perfect blend of scientist and entrepreneur. He liked coaching student entrepreneurs, and he and I started a *Shark Tank*-like pitch event where students competed for startup seed funds. Like Boom, Dan was not a conformist and liked to challenge the status quo.

One year, the three of us attended an educational conference in Austin, Texas. In between sessions, we spent lunch breaks and dinners discussing ideas and challenging each other on how we could create more disruptive educational experiences. One evening, we even talked about founding an entrepreneurial education company that would disrupt the staler models of higher education.

When I was around Dan and Boom, I was at my best. My energy was positive, and my mind was filled with possibility. I wasn't anxious or self-conscious. I felt more capable and more excited about the future. Simply put, I was happy and content with who I was. They appreciated me and what I was able to share and contribute to their conversations. They invited me to be part of initiatives, grants, research, and exciting new projects. If ever I was in my "flow" energy, as psychologist Mihaly Csikszentmihalyi terms it, it was when I was working with them.

Perhaps you have had colleagues like this. They set the bar high when it came to the way they showed up, the energy they brought into a room or project, and the type of people they were. Imagine if you made a point to surround yourself with these types of people more often. People who challenge you in a positive and supportive way. People who see the best in the world and inspire you to do the same. People who talk about ideas and not about others. People who dream big.

I've had my share of negative entrainment examples too. There have been times I found myself around critical and gossipy people. When that happened, I became increasingly anxious, critical, and negative myself. I entrained with that energy. I didn't like it; it didn't feel good. And I didn't like who I had become when I entrained with that crowd.

A good exercise we can do right away is to notice what types of energy and people we are entraining with. Who do we spend our time with? How does this impact our mood, emotions, outlook, and behavior? All of this is within our ability to control and to change. It may not be easy. And it may require difficult decisions. You may be thinking: What happens if I can't remove certain individuals from my daily life? Well, another option is that *you* can become the dominant energy and set a more productive frequency with which they can then entrain.

CREATING POSITIVE ENERGY BY CONTROLLING OUR EMOTIONAL STATE

How do we generate this positive energy? By changing our own internal energetic frequency. You might think this is about how we present ourselves to other people—how we speak and our body language. It's easy to say something incongruent with the energy we are feeling at the time, but this goes far beyond the superficial. It's about changing our energy at its root. The tools I'll share can be used in a variety of situations and conversations. This is where we can start to understand the depth of control we have over our interactions, our environments, and how we show up.

By far the greatest energy force in our bodies emanates from our heart. HeartMath® Institute is a nonprofit organization that has developed science-based tools to help people reduce stress and anxiety and increase their overall resilience and inner peace. In their leading publication, *The Science of the Heart*, the authors explain how our hearts emit an electromagnetic frequency that is three feet in diameter and can be measured by instruments (magnetometer). Our entire body vibrates to certain frequencies, and those frequencies are influenced by our emotions and our thought patterns. This impacts our heart rate variability (HRV), or the variation of time between our heartbeats. HRV is different from heart rate because HRV measures what happens between heartbeats.

When we are in a state of ease and inner peace, we have strong HRV, meaning the variability between beats is greater and more elastic. When we are stressed, anxious, or tense, our HRV is weak, and the variance between beats contracts. HeartMath® describes these as coherent and noncoherent states. When we are in a coherent state, our HRV shows a nice, fluid range of motion. When in an incoherent state, the range is tighter, more jagged, and inconsistent.

HeartMath® refers to emotions that create coherent states of ease as renewing emotions, such as gratitude, appreciation, love, joy, and compassion, among others. Those emotions that create incoherent, negative states are referred to as depleting emotions, such as anger, anxiety, fear, distrust, and frustration.

There's an evolutionary reason why we may tend toward incoherent, negative states. Recall that our brains are designed to be on the lookout for potential threats because a state of happiness or contentment could lower our guard against dangers that could harm us. If we do nothing to change how our system naturally responds to the world, then we may find ourselves frequently "on guard" and feeding those more negative thought patterns, anxieties, and worries.

Over time, this can reset our baseline. You may know people who seem to move through the world in a heightened state of agitation, frustration, or negativity. They may not even be aware that they show up this way, yet to those who have a calmer and more coherent baseline, it is readily apparent. Over time, a heightened and more anxious baseline takes a physical toll on the body.

Our HRV impacts the energy field around us and, whether we know it or not, it can then energetically influence the space and people in our orbit. I'm sure we've all had this experience. Your boss or coworker comes into the office and is running late. They are frantically looking through their calendar for the next appointment. Their voice has an anxious and hurried tone to it, and, before you know it, the people around them are also tense and on edge.

Now, imagine an outsider walking into that space who had not observed the few frantic seconds prior. They are walking into an HRV energy field fueled by anxiety and frustration. Their own heart will sense it even before they know what has happened. This can then impact their mood and outlook. The cycle continues to repeat. This is why the energy a leader brings into the room is so important. It sets the tone for others and the frequency with which the group will entrain. Just like the metronomes.

We have an incredible amount of control over our emotional states once we understand what drives them. We can then deploy the tools necessary to take back control so we see better outcomes. The key is learning how we can enhance our coherent states and quickly shift out of incoherent states when we find ourselves in them. We may not always have control over what is thrown at us day-to-day, but we have total control over our reaction to it. When we understand how we can control our responses, we can gain greater control over our lives.

We know that our emotional states affect our HRV, which has a direct impact on our health and on the people and situations around us. There's an inward response and an outward one because our heart radiates energy congruent with our emotional state. If we can learn to control this baseline reaction—the HRV—we can control our emotional state. The more we can reset that baseline to positive and coherent states, the more we can build up our resilience so we don't react in negative or damaging ways.

This is so important for leaders who manage the interpersonal dynamics of their teams while also needing to meet goals and deliver results. A missed deadline, an unexpected conflict between personnel, or a lower-than-expected financial forecast can send them into a tailspin. Yet, having the ability to positively respond and physically reset the system makes for more effective leaders and healthier organizations.

But how can we do this in practice?

Now, we've probably all heard about the importance of

breathing and taking slower breaths to calm ourselves down. First responders and athletes learn this in training. Sometimes it's called box breathing or slow breathing. HeartMath® calls it heart-focused breathing. So, why does this work? What's going on with our breathing that holds the key to better controlling our emotions?

A 2020 study in the *Harvard Business Review*, by Emma Seppälä, Christina Bradley, and Michael R. Goldstein entitled "Why Breathing Is So Effective at Reducing Stress" explains that, when we are in a high-stress situation, it's challenging to try to talk or reason ourselves out of it. The reason for this is that our prefrontal cortex—or rational brain—goes off-line. Our entire system is focused on survival, so it shuts off our executive functions to conserve energy. And, with that goes our creativity, our ability to evaluate alternate perspectives, and our capacity to think clearly to propose solutions.

Our emotional states correspond to different respiratory patterns and sequences. There's a feedback loop going on between our breathing and our emotions. If we change one, it will then impact the other. This is why Amy Cuddy's power posing works. It changes the very chemicals flowing through our body, so we feel and experience different emotions.

The problem is, many of us don't do this body and breathing work in the moment when we need to do it the most. We stay stuck in our heads, arguing or defending why we feel the way we do, wondering who is responsible for the emotion we are experiencing and insisting that if only a person or situation would change, we would feel better. That's an external locus. An internal locus says, "I can change my posture and my breath, and thereby improve my emotional state. Then, from a more coherent and positive state, I can make better decisions."

ACTIVITY: POSITIVE EMOTION RESET

The most effective action we can take when we find ourselves in a negative emotional state is to quickly shift out of that state. It won't help to analyze or dwell on the situation. We simply need to change our emotional state, and we can do that quickly by changing our physiology, and thereby altering the chemicals in our blood and the variability in our heartrate. This is how we gain control from the inside out.

Here's a tool I use when I'm in a stressful situation or I find my mind generating worrisome or fearful thoughts:

> Stand or sit up straight (standing up straight is preferred, but if you are in a place where you can't stand, then sit up straight.) Close your eyes and immediately call up a loving, warm, joyful memory of someone you love and who loves you. Activate all of your senses. Visualize what you saw, remember what you heard, smell any smells that were there, and feel the intensity and closeness of their embrace. Focus on this moment and notice feelings of warmth and appreciation fill up your entire body as you breathe slowly in and then out. After a minute or two, notice the change in your body and in how you feel. Now, open your eyes and return to the present moment renewed and recharged to face whatever situation or event that's before you.

While you may still have a problem to resolve, or a challenging conversation to have, you will have just optimized your entire system to find a successful solution. Moreover, you shifted yourself into a restored and more coherent state in the process. Long-term, the more we train our systems to operate this way, the more positive and restorative an environment we create for our cells, and thereby improve our overall physical health.

CHAPTER 7

THE THRIVE FRAMEWORK: TAKING BACK CONTROL

If you've made it this far in the book, then you probably understand locus of control much better than you did before. By now, you know that I firmly believe everyone has the ability to strengthen their internal locus and gain control over more aspects of their lives than they may have previously thought possible.

We are responsible for the outcomes in our lives and the successes or setbacks we experience, despite what takes place around us. We have control over what we decide experiences mean to us, for us, and what we do because of them. It's not the events of our lives that determine our destiny, it's the way we think about those events. And that's where we have a choice.

However, even if we understand how our locus of control works, there's still the problem of changing our subconscious beliefs and behavior patterns that operate as the magnet to our compass, disrupting the goals and outcomes we want to achieve. So, I wanted to design a process that incorporates what I learned and that can effect deep change quickly.

DEVELOPING THE **THRIVE** FRAMEWORK

In 2018, I developed a six-part framework that I call THRIVE. At first, I designed this for myself, as my own personal change-work framework. I then quickly began sharing it with colleagues, students, and entrepreneurs who I had been working with. The goal of THRIVE is to effect deep and lasting change because it works at the subconscious level. It recodes the magnet mind. The six aspects of the framework are based on principles from neuroscience, psychology, and theories of learning and development. Each one has a scientific basis for how and why it works.

I use this framework and have seen significant change in key areas of my life. THRIVE shifted the way I interact with my family and close friends. While I don't relish tough conversations or conflict, I'm able to navigate them with a greater sense of peace and resolve. I don't become physically sick from the anxiety surrounding them. I also noticed my relationships improving dramatically. Actions or inactions that would have triggered me before don't even phase me. For example, I recently declined attending a family gathering and one of my relatives commented that they never see me and that I had become a stranger. Objectively, I took note of the comment, yet it didn't ping me in that place that would have previously generated a defensive emotion. At work, I notice myself less angst-filled if a colleague is upset with a decision or a policy. Something in me doesn't take it as personally as I would have before my work with THRIVE. And, without consciously deciding to stop drinking soda and eating chocolate ice cream (sometimes half a pint every night), I found myself choosing healthier foods and eating more reasonable portions. Simply put, I feel more in control of my life.

This got me thinking. I wonder if this framework may have an impact on my locus of control? I decided to test it.

First, I had my beta group. This was hardly a random sample, as I started with folks I knew and who would be willing to do this exercise for two weeks—family, coworkers, and friends. While I shared the tool with about 20 individuals, only around seven did the activity and stuck with it for two full weeks. They all reported noticeable changes. They described feeling more in control of their time and their reactions to other people and events. Many mentioned how new and exciting opportunities came up for them that seemed far beyond coincidence. While this positive anecdotal feedback was reassuring, it wasn't objective or focused enough to know if I was on to something.

Next, I designed a study. I wanted to see if my framework could move the needle on someone's internal locus of control orientation. It was important that I measured where someone was on the internal locus continuum as the goal was to strengthen their internal index score. Now, Rotter's locus of control instrument gave a more binary result—either internal or external—so this wasn't ideal for my study. Therefore, I chose another locus of control instrument: Patricia Duttweiler's Internal Locus of Control Index. Duttweiler's instrument, first published in 1984, is an inventory of 28 questions that have been researched and tested. I should note that my pilot study was just that, a pilot. My goal was to see if my theory had value—if this tool could positively influence internal locus of control.

After securing the proper institutional review board approvals for my study, I began to recruit participants. Some 15 people opted in from a sample of around 500. None of the participants were friends or related to me. They knew me only through subscribing to an email list I had created from an interview series I had done around mindset, psychology, and successful leadership. None of them had in-depth knowledge of the concept of locus of control, nor did they have any prior exposure to the THRIVE framework tool that I would be testing.

The participants all anonymously took Duttweiler's self-report inventory. Then, for approximately three weeks, the 15 participants committed to using the THRIVE framework at a specific time each day, every day. I provided them with a series of step-by-step videos and a workbook to follow. Then, at the end of the time period, they once again took the 28-question inventory. I also asked them to provide qualitative feedback on what they experienced and felt during and after using THRIVE. The results were extraordinary.

After measuring the pre- and post-course scores, we saw a statistically significant increase in their internal locus of control identification. What was even better were their qualitative comments. I won't share them in too much detail here, yet many said they saw immediate shifts in their mood and also in the quality of their relationships. They reported feeling more focused and having more clarity with their work, as well as less anxiety or overwhelm during their day. They saw noticeable and significant shifts in how they felt about themselves and others. One person reported she felt better physically while doing THRIVE, and another said she had been more at peace and less stressed at work. The results were affirming. I thank my focus group participants. They were pioneers with me on this THRIVE journey, and I enjoyed getting to know them.

At this point, you may be wondering exactly what this framework is and how it works in practice. Below, I'll explain the core components and how to use them.

SETTING YOUR THREE GOALS

THRIVE stands for six powerful propulsion systems of the subconscious mind. It isn't based on completely novel or earth-shattering concepts. Rather, it pulls together established research and methodologies into a focused framework that can bring about fast and noticeable change.

Having now read through this book, you will recognize why each of these are so important.

Before we begin the actual practice of THRIVE, we will first identify three key objectives. I refer to this as calibrating our locus compass. These are the conscious goals we want to have in our lives right now. For the purposes of this activity, try to avoid overanalyzing or worrying about whether you can actually have them right now, or if they are even possible. The beauty of this exercise is that it's not rational, and that's exactly why it works.

Select a goal in each of the key areas of your life—wealth, relationships, and health.

Let's look at wealth first. This can be a specific number if you wish, like earning $100,000 per year, or having a net worth of $2 million. You can also state this qualitatively, like having financial freedom, or growing various sources of income every month.

I believe that giving our brains a numeric goal is important. This is not because money is important as an end goal. It's not. It's just numbers on a screen. It only has value in terms of what it provides for us; the opportunities it creates to be generous and share it in the world. Yet money has been a standard measurement our brains have understood for centuries. There's an evolutionary meaning inside our subconscious minds passed down from generations prior. Let's use this to our advantage.

Next, think of a relationship or family-related goal. Perhaps you're single and want to be in a relationship, or perhaps your current relationship is struggling and you want to improve it. Your goal could be that you have a loving relationship that grows stronger every day. We'll cover how to craft the goal in a minute.

Finally, let's move on to health and well-being. This can relate to spiritual health, mental health, or physical health. We are physical, mental, and spiritual beings moving through this world, so we want to be healthy and at peace with ourselves and each other.

Many people have asked if they can have a fourth goal because they sometimes feel they want to add more of a faith-based or spiritual objective. This is absolutely okay, although I recommend beginning with three first to keep it simple and focused. As you master this framework, adding a fourth goal is workable.

How to write these goals? This is where following the framework becomes very important. First, the subconscious mind understands one moment in time—right now. It doesn't care about what you *will* do, or *might* do, or *hope* to do. It pays attention to what is happening now because its job is to be focused on what could help or harm you in the moment. That is its survival mechanism.

Many times, we have been taught to write affirmations or statements in the future tense. For example: "I will attract abundance and become financially free." This feels great to our conscious mind because it makes rational sense. Sure, we don't have it now, yet it's possible we can have it later. Yet our subconscious mind is thinking: Great, nudge me when that's actually happening. It's not something I'm going to worry about or focus on right now. So, to create a sense of urgency, we want to write our goal statements *as if* they are happening now. For this purpose, use present tense or present progressive. For example: "Every day, I give generously in my relationship with (name of your partner or person you want to deepen your relationship with) and we are growing closer," or "Every day, I am building my physical fitness and eating nutritious foods."

Again, don't worry about whether you believe you are doing this or not, or if you just downed a bag of Fritos before reading this section of the book. This is not the time to have your rational brain get in the way. Thank it for its faith in you (not!) and then let it slip off to the side while you continue this exercise.

Next, positive wording. We need to focus on what we *want* to do and not on what we don't. The subconscious mind has an odd way of hearing "don't" or "won't" statements. You know how children have a tendency to do exactly what they are told not to do? You say, "Don't push the red button," as their eyes fixate on it, and it's all you can do to hold them back. You say, "Don't eat that cupcake," as their guilty expression reveals they cannot wait to stick their fingers into the frosting as soon as you're not looking. Their mind hears, "Push the red button," and, "Eat cake," before it hears *don't*.

Similarly, our subconscious mind is prone to want what it cannot have if it hears these phrases. We need to talk to it in simple, focused words. Rather than a goal of *not* eating junk food, our goal will be that we eat only healthy and nourishing foods. Rather than *not* fighting with our family, our goal would be that we develop loving, caring, and nurturing relationships with our loved ones. See the trick?

Now that we are minding our p's (positive wording and present/present progressive tense), we can begin to construct our three goals. Here are some examples of goal statements

I've used myself and with the leaders and entrepreneurs I've worked with:

- "I attract healthy, supportive, and inspiring people into my life."
- "Every day, I am making healthy and nourishing food choices."
- "I give and receive authentic and connected love."
- "I see abundance and financial freedom all around me."
- "I have a healthy and strong mind and body."
- "I am financially free."

STARTING THE THRIVE PROCESS: SIX DRIVERS OF CHANGE

It's now time to get your pen and paper ready. Make sure you have ample supply, because it's amazing how easy it can be to lose your pen or run out of paper. In fact, I would encourage you to buy a nicely packaged and bound writing journal. You can even order a copy of the accompanying THRIVE Journal online and use this to help you structure the process.

Place it on your nightstand, as close to your bed as you can. If you don't have a nightstand, consider sleeping with it under your pillow or placing it on the floor right next to your bed. You'll need a pen beside it too.

Let's get started with the THRIVE part of the process, and you'll see why it's so important to have the journal close by your bed.

THRIVE is an acronym that stands for timing, handwriting, repetition, imagination, visualization, and emotion.

- Timing
- Handwriting
- Repetition (law of compounding)

- Imagination
- Visualization
- Emotion

T Is for Timing

Let's start with timing. As discussed in Chapter 4, we know that our brain's ability to take in, download, and learn new information is at its strongest when we are young and operating from the lower brain wave states: delta, alpha, and theta. We need to access those lower brain wave states in the THRIVE process.

This may feel very counterintuitive to many of us, particularly now that we are adults. We like to think we learn when we read, study, analyze, or create. Of course, we do, yet this is a different type of learning. The learning we are talking about here enables us to get inside our subconscious magnet mind and encode the beliefs and the meanings we want to in order to move our lives forward. There are two times in any day where our brains naturally pass into and out of these lower-wave states or deep-learning states. One time is right when we wake up, and the other is as we fall asleep.

Because the THRIVE activity requires that we consciously commit to performing this activity and because we need to do it before we enter into these deep-learning states, we will use the time portal right before we go to sleep. You will write your three goal statements within 15 minutes of going to sleep.

Now, why 15 minutes? Think about anything you do, read, think about, or say right before you go to sleep. Have you noticed these thoughts tend to manifest in your dreams? A movie or news story you watched before bed, or a social media post you read on your phone, or a conversation you had with someone in the evening. Why does this happen?

As thoughts, images, or ideas enter our mind, they can reside for up to 50 minutes in our conscious mind before it filters, distorts, or deletes what is in there based on our beliefs or biases about ourselves and the world. Yet, when we go to sleep, the conscious mind lets go. It has to, or we don't actually fall asleep. And, as it does that, the thoughts, images, ideas, or stories that have just come into our brain fall directly into our subconscious magnet mind. They have less time and less chance of being filtered or deleted to match our established map of the world. This way, we don't have to fight the conscious mind or any of its beliefs that run counter to what we want to put inside of it.

I liken this timing portal to the legend of the Trojan horse. Rather than fight the army, the conscious mind, at the gate, we can place new learnings in our mind within a particular time window so that they can sail right in when the conscious mind is off-line, just like the Trojan horse sailed into the city when the gates were down.

Imagine if we shrunk this timing window. Instead of 50 minutes, we will aim for 15 minutes before we go to sleep. This means finishing your nightly routine before you do THRIVE. Brush your teeth, put on your pajamas, set aside your cell phone. The last point is so important; you do not want to be reading the news online or scrolling social media before you go to sleep. That will have the opposite effect you want to achieve with THRIVE. And, yes, it's okay if you fall asleep in 20 or 30 minutes. Of course, it's even better if you fall asleep within five or 10 minutes. We just want to get that timing portal window as close as possible to when you actually fall asleep to increase the strength and intensity with which the new goal statements drop into the subconscious mind.

H Is for Handwriting

Next is handwriting. Handwriting is an ideomotor activity. It has a direct communication line into our nervous system. When we handwrite words, they have a way of landing more firmly within our subconscious mind. And they stick. Think about how, if we write something down, we tend to remember it, even if we don't ever refer back to it. Or perhaps you've heard highly successful people talk about how they write down their goals? They don't just say them, or think them, they write them.

Handwriting activates and engages our nervous system in the process of learning. There's also an entire body of research around handwriting analysis, which links it to the subconscious. Psychologists can use the handwriting of criminals to analyze what is going on in their subconscious mind and to evaluate or predict criminal pathology. It reveals something about their personality and desires, even if those facts are well hidden by the criminals themselves.

In this process, the connection will be working in the opposite direction. Your handwritten goals will be directly talking to your subconscious mind. For this step of the framework, you will handwrite each of your goals three times. You may write each one out three times, then move on to the next, or you can write them each out, one by one, then repeat the sequence, and again. Do whichever option feels right to you.

R Is for Repetition

Our subconscious mind will eventually automate what we repeatedly do. **Repetition** is interesting because it's how we learn things when we are around age six or seven, after we have moved out of the deeper-learning brain wave states. Think about how we learned vocabulary or mathematical problems. And now, even as adults, the more frequently we hear, see, read, or are exposed to something, the more familiar it becomes.

Repetition penetrates the conscious mind wall over time. As we repeat an action, it compounds, making the learning even stronger. This is how new habits are formed. Our brain notices we are doing something over and over again and says, "This must be important. Let's automate this process." So, we will use repetition in the THRIVE framework by undertaking the same process every night.

I Is for Imagination

Our subconscious does not distinguish between what is real and what we vividly **imagine**. Sports psychologists have known this for years. Vividly imagining ourselves in a scene, situation, or outcome that we want programs the magnet mind that this is known, familiar, accepted, and expected. When something in our magnet mind is considered familiar and accepted, our five senses perceive and sort information as if this imagined state is happening to us now.

We will attract new opportunities, people, and events into our lives that align with what we are imagining. Now engage all of your five senses as you form the image of your ideal state. In this way, we begin to make the imagined world come to life so we can connect more fully with it.

Richard Sheridan, author of *Joy, Inc.*, and *Chief Joy Officer*, cofounder and chief storyteller at Menlo Innovations, a software design and development firm in Ann Arbor, Michigan, once told me that he *saw* Menlo's headquarters a decade before he started the company. He was walking in Ann Arbor and vividly imagined Menlo Innovations having an office in the heart of downtown. He imagined what it would look, feel, and sound like.

It's tempting for us to hear that and think: That's a nice story, but imagining something doesn't create it out of thin air. But, to a certain extent, it did. Sheridan programmed his magnet mind with the reality he wanted to see and saw it as if it were happening to him in the moment. This helped to create the opportunities and events that led up to Menlo's founding. When you activate your imagination, make sure to engage all of your senses, and literally transport yourself to your imagined world. Let your mind stay there and take it all in.

V Is for Visualization

Visualization is an excellent tool to use as you are imagining your ideal outcome. It helps intensify the focus of the imagination and locks our magnet mind on the target of our goals. It sets the coordinates of the compass. Visualize achieving the goals you have and living the life you want. What will it look like when you have it? Picture every aspect with clarity and detail.

If you want to earn $200,000 per year, visualize what you would do with the money. How would you live, shop, and eat? Visualize how you would make the money, what your work would look like, and what car and house you might have.

E Is for Emotion

The last step in the THRIVE framework is to activate the **emotions** associated with what you are imagining and visualizing. They are the emotions you feel as you are living in these experiences. This might be joy, exuberance, happiness, awe, or satisfaction. Bring up any and all feelings that emerge from this process.

Allow yourself to slip into this emotional state as if you are experiencing the actualization of your goals in the immediate moment. You can cycle through each of your goal statements, imagining them, visualizing, and then allowing the emotions associated with them to come up. Feel them fully, as if you are truly immersed in this new reality; as if you have traveled to the place and space where this ideal state exists. Allow this flood of positive emotions to flow through your mind and body. And then, close your journal, put down your pen, turn out the lights, and go to sleep. That's all you have to do; your magnet mind will take care of the rest.

CONSISTENCY AND COMMITMENT

The entire THRIVE framework takes five minutes or less every night. When you begin, you may find it takes longer, especially as you focus on writing out your goal statements three times each. It may also take time to practice imagining, visualizing, and then activating the positive emotions.

What does it take to see results? Of course, I cannot make any guarantees, legally or otherwise. I cannot guarantee any particular result with health, finances, or relationships. I can tell you about the incredible results the THRIVE focus group experienced in the three weeks they used this tool in terms of their work, relationships, and health. I can also tell you about the entrepreneurs who used this and saw their businesses take off, or the leaders who were struggling with overwhelm and anxiety and were able to reduce their stress and enhance their productivity, or the psychologist who uses this framework with his clients to help realize real change.

What these experiences and many others taught me is that

there are two things that are required to see results: consistency and commitment.

Consistency and commitment mean you do THRIVE every night before you go to sleep and you don't stop when you feel resistance from your magnet mind. You have to be massively committed to your goals and to having those in your life right now. Many times, people will begin THRIVE, do it for a few days, then stop. They will report noticing changes in the first few days and then stop once they get the hang of it. They might say, "I got this, it works, okay great." Or perhaps they will lose their pen or run out of paper.

It's amazing how many seemingly rational reasons our brain can create to stop doing something when it feels new shifts inside us that are unfamiliar at first (and perhaps unsettling). Missing a night here or there won't remove the positive changes you experience, of course, but this is an ongoing practice. Think of it like working out or eating healthily. It needs to happen often to build momentum and create change.

Regularity is particularly important when it comes to the magnet mind, and here's why: Some thought, worry, fear, or idea will drop into your subconscious each day and night. It's just how it works. And if we are not actively telling it what we want to experience, then the default system kicks in. The default system is what we had before, what didn't work, and what we don't want. It's skewed toward the negative or anxious. That is the reality.

Consistent practice will shift us toward where we want to go by instead placing what we want inside our subconscious. That's why it's so important to push through and do THRIVE every single night. After about a month, it will come so naturally to you that you won't have to focus on consistency and commitment. It will be as automatic as brushing your teeth before bed.

One useful method to increase consistency with THRIVE is to use habit stacking, a practice James Clear talks about in his 2018 book, *Atomic Habits: An Easy & Proven Way to Build Good Habits & Break Bad Ones.* Steve Scott also expanded on this concept in his book, *Habit Stacking: 97 Small Life Changes That Take Five Minutes or Less.*

Habit stacking is when you add a habit, or several smaller habits, right before or after an existing and established routine. In essence, the existing habit or routine, which has become much more automatic, is the trigger to remember to undertake the new habit.

For example, you may do THRIVE right before or after you brush your teeth or set your alarm. The goal is to make sure the new practice is grouped together with existing habits that you always carry out so that you increase your chances of making the new habit part of your existing routine.

THRIVE is effective because its six elements act like the propulsion systems of our magnet mind. It sneaks in through the back door, working on a subconscious level, rather than trying to change our conscious beliefs, which have a much weaker influence on our behavior. This was likely the change that my locus of control focus group saw in their own internal locus scores after doing the THRIVE framework every day. They not only increased their internal locus of control scores, but they also felt more in control of their lives, their emotions, and their day-to-day results.

And, more importantly, it's effective because it's simple. It relies only on our ability to do each of the six steps and to commit to doing them consistently.

MORNING MINDSET MASTERY

As a bonus activity to doing your THRIVE framework, you can do a brief morning activity as soon as you wake up. You may use the same THRIVE journal you used from the night before, or, if you obtain a copy of my published THRIVE Journal, there's guidance in there to help you complete this Morning Mindset activity. While we do THRIVE each night, it's important we begin our day in a positive frame of mind. This is referred to as "priming" our brains to perceive and filter information in the very best and most useful light for us throughout the day. It is a conscious mind activity, so it can be done when we are awake and ready to start our day.

Begin by writing down three things you are grateful for each morning. This can be a relationship with a family member, significant other, friend, or colleague. It could be your health and well-being. Or it might be a wonderful celebration or event that just took place. As you write, allow feelings of gratitude and peace to flow throughout your mind and body.

Here are some examples:

I am grateful for my sister.
I am grateful for meaningful work each day.
I am grateful for my supportive friends.

Research shows that feelings of gratitude and appreciation release natural healthy hormones in our body and especially into our bloodstream. These calm and center us and make us more likely to navigate challenges in a more resilient and positive manner. It feels good when we experience gratitude, *and* it's good for us.

Unlike with the THRIVE framework, you don't need to write each of the morning gratitude statements three times. Writing them once and allowing the positive emotions and feelings to flow through your body will prime your mind for greater productivity and resilience throughout your day. It is my hope that the material in this book, the THRIVE framework, and the Morning Mindset priming activity will help you take control and accomplish your goals!

EPILOGUE

THE TAPESTRY OF LIFE

It's my hope that this book can help you better understand and strengthen your internal locus of control, and perhaps even build, what I call, a strong locus mindset. Having a locus mindset means we recognize that we are in control of our lives, even if we don't always *feel* like we are. We control our locus.

The negative thought and behavior patterns we often find ourselves in are the result of the beliefs that have been encoded at a very early age. They have so much power because our young brains are so susceptible, and our survival instincts can shape our memories and the familiar patterns we seek.

By grasping how our subconscious works, and how the dominant beliefs we formed about ourselves and the world aren't always based in reality, we gain the ability to change our thoughts and behaviors. If we do not go inside ourselves to do the work, we continue to move through the world on autopilot—stuck in our ways, determined our viewpoint is always the correct one, and never fully able to move beyond repetitive and destructive life patterns. By doing the intense personal development needed to get real and lasting change, we can take back control and change our lives for the better. I hope this book has provided useful information and tools to help you on the path to self-improvement and self-empowerment. We are all on this continual journey.

I want to share one final reflection. For years, I thought about how my mistakes, struggles, and the ways my own perceived lack of control over my life hurt not only myself but others as well. The years I went not connecting with my sister, my parents, or my family. The pain I caused my husband because I was blind to the wounds I needed to heal from my past—a past that was spent in dramatic and emotionally unhealthy relationships trying to fill voids of self-worth based on insecurity and doubt. I wished so much that I could have figured out all of this sooner and changed myself for the better. I felt like I burned up so much time, energy, and lost opportunity.

Then I remembered another one of my favorite *Star Trek* episodes, "Tapestry." Captain Picard ends up in sick bay after suffering fatal injuries that cause his artificial heart to stop. The ever-powerful and mysterious character known as Q then appears to give Picard a second chance at life and an opportunity to go back in time to change one regret that he has.

Since Picard's fatal injury was to his heart, he chooses the event that injured his original heart years ago. The episode shows a young Picard engaged in a bar fight with a much larger and stronger opponent who drives a sword through the younger Picard's heart. In theory, by changing this one event, it would spare him the failure of his artificial one decades later and save his life in the present time. However, an interesting change occurs. In the alternate life, Picard does not become a captain. He ends up staying a junior science officer and has a boring and mediocre career.

That one event, although seemingly negative, had actually altered the trajectory of his life in a positive way. Q returns him unharmed to his original timeline after having given him a glimpse of this important lesson. Reflecting on this experience, Picard explains his life regrets as loose threads in a quilt. While at times he might wish he could go back, sew these up, or pull them out, he realizes this would unravel the entire tapestry of his life.

I've often thought about this episode in relation to my own life, and perhaps this is helpful for you too. As much as we have regrets, and situations that we wished we handled differently, these events are all part of who we have become today. They are part of our tapestry—the very fabric of our present and our future. Nothing is ever wasted. While we would never wish to repeat our mistakes or hurt ourselves or others in the process, where we are now is the unique sum of those experiences. It's our own tapestry and may very well hold the key to a greater life purpose. In changing our own lives for the better we can use our journey and experiences to help others and positively change the world around us.

DUTTWEILER'S INTERNAL CONTROL INDEX

Please read each statement. Where there is a blank _____, decide what your normal or usual attitude, feeling, or behavior would be:

- A. **Rarely** (less than 10% of the time)
- B. **Occasionally** (about 30% of the time)
- C. **Sometimes** (about half of the time)
- D. **Frequently** (about 70% of the time)
- E. **Usually** (more than 90% of the time)

Of course, there are always unusual situations in which this would not be the case, but think of what you would do or feel in most normal situations.

Write the letter that describes your usual attitude or behavior.

1. When faced with a problem I _____ try to forget it.
2. I _____ need frequent encouragement from others for me to keep working at a difficult task.
3. I _____ like jobs where I can make decisions and be responsible for my own work.
4. I _____ change my opinion when someone I admire disagrees with me.
5. If I want something I _____ work hard to get it.
6. I _____ prefer to learn the facts about something from someone else rather than have to dig them out for myself.
7. I will _____ accept jobs that require me to supervise others.

8. I _____ have a hard time saying "no" when someone tries to sell me something I don't want.
9. I _____ like to have a say in any decisions made by any group I'm in.
10. I _____ consider the different sides of an issue before making any decisions.
11. What other people think _____ has a great influence on my behavior.
12. Whenever something good happens to me I _____ feel it is because I've earned it.
13. I _____ njoy being in a position of leadership.
14. I _____ need someone else to praise my work before I am satisfied with what I've done.
15. I _____ am sure enough of my opinions to try and influence others.
16. When something is going to affect me I _____ learn as much about it as I can.
17. I _____ decide to do things on the spur of the moment.
18. For me, knowing I've done something well is _____ more important than being praised by someone else.
19. I _____ let other people's demands keep me from doing things I want to do.
20. I _____ stick to my opinions when someone disagrees with me.
21. I _____ do what I feel like doing not what other people think I ought to do.
22. I _____ get discouraged when doing something that takes a long time to achieve results.
23. When part of a group I _____ prefer to let other people make all the decisions.

24. When I have a problem I _____ follow the advice of friends or relatives.
25. I _____ enjoy trying to do difficult tasks more than I enjoy trying to do easy tasks.
26. I _____ prefer situations where I can depend on someone else's ability rather than just my own.
27. Having someone important tell me I did a good job is _____ more important to me than feeling I've done a good job.
28. When I'm involved in something I _____ try to find out all I can about what is going on even when someone else is in charge.

Scoring

The Internal Control Index consists of 28 items with response alternatives that fall along a 5-point scale from (A) "rarely" to (E) "usually." The items are worded so that highly internal-oriented subjects are expected to answer half of the questions at the "usually" end of the scale and the other half at the "rarely" end of the scale. The appropriate internal response is valued at 5. The opposite response alternative—appropriate to an external-oriented subject—is valued at 1.

The response (A) is valued at 5 for items 1, 2, 4, 6, 8, 11, 14, 17, 19, 22, 23, 24, 26, and 27.

The response (E) is scored 5 for items 3, 5, 7, 9, 10, 12, 13, 15, 16, 18, 20, 21, 25, and 28.

Other responses (B, C, D) are not attributed points.

A maximum high internal response pattern would result in a score of 140. A minimum low internal response pattern would result in a score of 28.

I am grateful to SAGE Publications, Inc., for allowing me to reproduce Duttweiler's Internal Control Index.

Duttweiler, P.C. The Internal Control Index: A Newly Developed Measure of Locus of Control. Educational and Psychological Measurement 44(2), pp. 209-221. Copyright © 1984 by Educational and Psychological Measurement. Reprinted by Permission of SAGE Publications, Inc.

THE THRIVE JOURNAL

I created the THRIVE Journal if you want an easy template to follow as you work your way through the THRIVE process. It's available via Amazon and it complements the content of this book.

Below are some samples from the journal to get you started on your journey. And, here are some example THRIVE goal statements that may inspire you as you work to create yours. Feel free to use any of these verbatim if you like them!

Health

I have a healthy and strong mind and body.
I eat clean, healthy, and nourishing foods.
I exercise daily.
My mind is strong, clear, and healthy.
Every day, my mental health becomes stronger.
I am an active and healthy person.
I have a calm, healthy, and clear mind.
Every day and in every way, I am achieving my ideal weight, body size, and shape.

Wealth

I attract abundance, wealth, and prosperity in all areas of my life.
I am financially free and give generously.
I earn income from new and different sources.
I give generously of my time, talents, and treasure.
Every day, my wealth and resources increase.

Relationships

I love and accept myself deeply and completely.
I am worthy of real love and am enough.
I am loved, cherished, and valued in my relationships.
I attract calm, peaceful, and healthy people and events into my life.
I give and receive intimate and connected love.
I pray daily and have a deep and committed relationship to my faith.
I am a caring and loving parent/partner/friend.

SAMPLE TEMPLATE FOR THE NIGHTLY THRIVE FRAMEWORK

Handwrite each of your three THRIVE goals three times each.

Health

1. _____

2. _____

3. _____

Wealth

1. _____

2. _____

3. _____

Relationships

1. _____

2. _____

3. _____

SAMPLE TEMPLATE FOR MORNING MINDSET MASTERY

When you wake up, write down three things you are grateful for in your life right now.

1. _____

2. _____

3. _____

ENDNOTES

CHAPTER 1

Rotter, J. B. (1966). Generalized expectancies for internal versus external control of reinforcement. *Psychological Monographs: General and Applied 80(1)*, 1–28. https://doi.org/10.1037/h0092976

Nguyen, S. (2013). Locus of control: Stop making excuses and start taking responsibility. Retrieved from WorkplacePsychology.com: https://workplacepsychology.wordpress.com/2013/06/05/locus-of-control-stop-making-excuses-and-start-taking-responsibility/

American Addiction Centers. Personal responsibility and locus of control. Retrieved from MentalHelp.Net: https://www.mentalhelp.net/addiction/personal-responsibility-and-locus-of-control/

Anderson, C. R. (1977). Locus of control, coping behaviors, and performance in a stress setting: A longitudinal study. *Journal of Applied Psychology 62(4)*, 446–451. https://doi.org/10.1037/0021-9010.62.4.446

Dumitriu, C., Timofti, J. C., Nechita, E., & Dumitriu, G. (2014). The influence of the locus of control and decision-making capacity upon the leadership style. *Procedia—Social and Behavioral Sciences* 141(494–499). https://doi:10.1016/j.sbspro.2014.05.086

Buddelmeyer, H., & Powdthavee, N. (2016). Can having internal locus of control insure against negative shocks? *Journal of Economic Behavior & Organization,* 122(88–109). https://doi.org/10.1016/j.jebo.2015.11.014

Klontz, B. T., Seay, M. C., Sullivan, P., & Canale, A. (2014). The psychology of wealth: Psychological factors associated with high income. *Journal of Financial Planning* 27 (12) 46–53.

Klontz, B. T., Sullivan, P., Seay, M. C., & Canale, A. (2015). The wealthy: A financial psychological profile. *Consulting Psychology Journal: Practice and Research* 67(2), 127–143. https://doi.org/10.1037/cpb0000027

Nowicki, S. (2016). *Choice or Chance: Understanding Your Locus of Control and Why It Matters.* Prometheus Books.

Duttweiler, P. C. The internal control index: A newly developed measure of locus of control. *Educational and Psychological Measurement* 44, 2 (June 1984): 209–221. https://doi.org/10.1177/0013164484442004

Bullers, S. & Prescott, C. A. (2007). An exploration of the independent contributions of genetics, shared environment, specific environment, and adult roles and statuses on perceived control. *Sociological Inquiry* 71(145–163). https://doi.org/10.1111/j.1475-682X.2001.tb01106.x

Scott, E. (2020). How to develop an internal locus of control. Retrieved from VerywellMind.com: https://www.verywellmind.com/develop-an-internal-locus-of-control-3144943

Tartakovsky, M. (2017). Cultivating an internal locus of control—and why it's crucial. Retrieved from https://psychcentral.com/blog/cultivating-an-internal-locus-of-control-and-why-its-crucial#role-in-your-life

CHAPTER 2

Szegedy-Maszak M. (2005). Mysteries of the mind. *U.S. news & world report*, 138(7), 52–61.

Berlin, H. A. (2014). The neural basis of the dynamic unconscious: Response to commentaries. *Neuropsychoanalysis* 13:1(63–71). https://doi/abs/10.1080/15294145.2011.10773663

Hardy, B. (2020). *Personality Isn't Permanent: Break Free from Self-Limiting Beliefs and Rewrite Your Story*. Portfolio/Penguin.

CHAPTER 4

Ball, D. and Keenan, D. (2009). *Reptile: The 2009 Manual of the Plaintiff's Revolution*. Balloon Press.

MacLean, P. D. (1990). *The Triune Brain in Evolution: Role in Paleocerebral Functions*. Plenum Press.

Barrett, L. F. (2017). *How Emotions Are Made: The Secret Life of the Brain*. Mariner.

Kahneman, D. (2011). *Thinking, Fast and Slow*. Farrar, Straus and Giroux.

Bungay Stanier, M. (2016). *The Coaching Habit: Say Less, Ask More & Change the Way You Lead Forever*. Box of Crayons Press.

Tierney, J. & Baumeister, R. (2019). *The Power of Bad: How the Negativity Effect Rules Us and How We Can Rule It*. Penguin.

CHAPTER 5

LeDoux, J. E. (1994). Emotion, memory and the brain. *Scientific American* 270(6), 50–57. https://doi.org/10.1038/scientificamerican0694-50

Burra, N. et al. (2013). Amygdala activation for eye contact despite complete cortical blindness. *Journal of Neuroscience* 33 (25) 10483–10489. https://doi.org/10.1523/JNEUROSCI.3994-12.2013

Alberini, C. M., LeDoux, J. E. (2013). Memory reconsolidation. *Current Biology* 9;23(17): R746–750. https://doi.org/10.1016/j.cub.2013.06.046

Ekman, P. (2007). *Emotions Revealed: Recognizing Faces and Feelings to Improve Communication and Emotional Life.* Henry Holt.

Schiller, D. et al. (2010). Preventing the return of fear in humans using reconsolidation update mechanisms. *Nature*, 463(7277), 49–53. https://doi.org/10.1038/nature08637

Ecker, B., Ticic, R., Hulley, L. (2012). *Unlocking the Emotional Brain: Eliminating Symptoms at Their Roots Using Memory Reconsolidation.* Routledge.

Kahneman, D. (2011). *Thinking, fast and slow.* Farrar, Straus and Giroux.

Baum, B. About holographic memory resolution. Healing Dimensions, ACC. Retrieved from: http://www.healingdimensions.com/.

CHAPTER 6

Ozanich, S. R. (2011). *The Great Pain Deception: Faulty Medical Advice Is Making Us Worse.* Waterside Productions.

van der Kolk, B. A. (2014). *The Body Keeps the Score: Brain, Mind, and Body in the Healing of Trauma.* Penguin.

Carney, D. R., Cuddy, A. J. C., & Yap, A. J. (2010). Power posing: Brief nonverbal displays affect neuroendocrine levels and risk tolerance. *Psychological Science* 21, 1363–1368. https://doi.org/10.1177/0956797610383437

Carney, D. R., Cuddy, A. J. C., & Yap, A. J. (2015). Review and summary of research on the embodied effects of expansive (vs. contractive) nonverbal displays. *Psychological Science* 26, 657–663. https://doi.org/10.1177/0956797614566855

Lipton, B. H. (2016). *The Biology of Belief: Unleashing the Power of Consciousness, Matter & Miracles:10th anniversary edition.* Hay House.

Gustafson C. (2017). Bruce Lipton, PhD: The Jump From Cell Culture to Consciousness. *Integrative medicine (Encinitas, Calif.)*, 16(6), 44–50.

Nijhout, H. F. (1990). Problems and Paradigms: Metaphors and the role of genes in development. *Bioessays.* Sep;12(9):441–446. https://doi.org.10.1002/bies.950120908

Roohafza, H. et al. (2016). Anxiety, depression and distress among irritable bowel syndrome and their subtypes: An epidemiological population based study. *Advanced Biomedical Research* 5, 183. https://doi.org.10.4103/2277-9175.190938

Chitkara, D. K. et al. (2008). Early life risk factors that contribute to irritable bowel syndrome in adults: A systematic review. *American Journal of Gastroenterology* 103(3), 765–775. https://doi.org.10.1111/j.1572-0241.2007.01722.x

Hay, L. (1991). *The Power Is Within You.* Hay House.

Hay, L. (1984). *Heal Your Body.* Hay House.

Abdolmanafi, A. et al. (2011). The moderating role of locus of control on the relationship between anger and depression in patients with major depression disorder. *Procedia—Social and Behavioral Sciences* 30, 297–301. https://doi.org/10.1016/j.sbspro.2011.10.059

Cvetanovski, J. & Jex, S. M. (1994). Locus of control of unemployed people and its relationship to psychological and physical well-being. *Work & Stress* 8:1, 60-67. https://doi.org/10.1080/02678379408259976

Wigger, E. (2011). Locus of control and cardiovascular health. Retrieved from UnhealthyWork.org: https://unhealthywork.org/psychological-risk-factors/locus-of-control-and-cardiovascular-health/

Powell, K. (2005). It's the ecology, stupid! *Nature* 435, 268–270. https://doi.org.10.1038/435268a

HeartMath® Institute. (2015). Science of the heart: Exploring the role of the heart in human performance. Vol. 2. HeartMath® Institute. Retrieved from heartmath.org: https://www.heartmath.org/research/science-of-the-heart/

HeartMath® Institute. (2012). *The Inside Story: Understanding the Power of Feelings.* HeartMath.

Seppala, E., Bradley, C., & Goldstein, M. R. (2020). Research: Why breathing is so effective at reducing stress. *Harvard Business Review.* Retrieved from hbr.org: https://hbr.org/2020/09/research-why-breathing-is-so-effective-at-reducing-stress

Cuddy, A. (2012). "Your body language may shape who you are." [Video] TED Conferences. https://www.ted.com/talks/amy_cuddy_your_body_language_may_shape_who_you_are?language=en

CHAPTER 7

Sheridan, R. (2013). Joy, Inc.: How We Build a Workplace People Love. Portfolio.

Clear, J. (2018). Atomic Habits: An Easy & Proven Way to Build Good Habits & Break Bad Ones. Avery.

Scott, S. J. (2014). Habit Stacking: 97 Small Life Changes That Take Five Minutes or Less. Oldtown Publishing.

ABOUT THE AUTHOR

Suzy Siegle is an educator and locus of control champion. An attorney and business coach, she loves helping high performing leaders and entrepreneurs plan new ventures, grow existing businesses and build thriving organizational cultures. Suzy is a member of the International Positive Psychology Association and the Center for Positive Organization's Community of Scholars at the University of Michigan's Ross School of Business.

She holds a bachelor's degree, a master of business administration, a juris doctor, and a doctorate in higher education leadership and management. She is a certified HeartMath® trainer, a certified executive coach through the center for executive coaching and has earned certifications in applied neuroscience and brain health, the neuroscience of learning and development, and consumer neuroscience and neuromarketing.

Made in the USA
Monee, IL
29 May 2023